T0149312

LIVING THE
AMERICAN
DREAM

PATRICIA A. JORDAN

WESTBOW
PRESS®
A DIVISION OF THOMAS NELSON
& ZONDERVAN

Author Credits: This is my second book. My first one, My Journey in Overcoming Dysthymic Depression was my first one.

This book is a work of non-fiction. Unless otherwise noted, the author and the publisher make no explicit guarantees as to the accuracy of the information contained in this book and in some cases, names of people and places have been altered to protect their privacy.

All Bible scripture verses are from the New Living Translation.

WestBow Press books may be ordered through booksellers or by contacting:

WestBow Press
A Division of Thomas Nelson & Zondervan
1663 Liberty Drive
Bloomington, IN 47403
www.westbowpress.com
1 (866) 928-1240

ISBN: 978-1-5127-7586-0 (sc)
ISBN: 978-1-5127-7587-7 (hc)
ISBN: 978-1-5127-7585-3 (e)

Library of Congress Control Number: 2017902640

Print information available on the last page.

WestBow Press rev. date: 3/17/2017

For my Parents:
May the story of your
Entrepreneurial success
Never be forgotten.

My parents, M. G. and June (Lloyd) Bell
in Knoxville, TN, 1946

SPECIAL THANKS

A special thank you to my husband Jeff. Thanks for loving me, believing in and supporting my writing projects. Your encouragement and enthusiasm have been essential to me. I'm not sure I would've gotten this project down on paper without you. I love you as much today as I did almost forty years ago.

A special thank you to each of my children Ruth, Rachel, and Esther. Each of you have made your dad and I proud of you. Plus, you three have added more to my life than what I could ever express on paper. But, here is my effort to do just that. I love you three and my two granddaughters, Mia and Isabelle beyond what words can express.

Thank you to my sisters Carol (Bell) Smith, and Deena (Bell) Long. You both have always been there for me. That means a lot to me. I love you both.

I appreciate my deceased brother "Gene" Bell taking time to take me to the old home sites, graveyards, so on.

Thanks to my cousin CPO (Ret) Ken Lloyd and his wonderful wife Bonnie Lloyd. Thank you for meeting me in Murphy. And for getting me connected to our relatives there. You both have helped to bring this project together. "I love y'all!"

I have written a special "Thank You" and a "Tribute" to my parents and my Aunt Jo near the end of this story. Each one of them helped me more than they realized in writing my book.

FOREWORD

For my birthday, this past May, my children provided me with a DNA kit from Ancestry.com. Then, on Father's Day they did the same for their dad, my husband Jeff. We followed the instructions and sent off our little vials of saliva. Then, we waited. Then, we got busy and kind of put it on the "back burner."

Finally, our results came in our email accounts. I knew it all along, I'm one hundred percent Celtic. And now I have proof of it. Well, kind of. We Celtic people have always liked to co-mingle. So, I'm a tad Mediterranean, a lot of Southern England, Irish and, a touch of Viking. My ancestors lived where ever the Celtic people have settled down and called home. That alone proves it for me.

The peaceful Celts spread their clans out from the Celtic Sea to the British Channel. Then to avoid war with the Angles (later Anglos) they crossed the mountains and settled down in Wales. Mountain life suited my Celtic ancestors, as it has my closes relatives and myself. As far I can count, there are eight generations of relatives that call the Great Smokey Mountains home.

My ancestral Celtic relatives loved Wales, and prospered there. Even today Welsh people still speak the ancient Celtic language. But, the early Celts like we have today, discovered that peace is hard to find.

Later they took their herds of cows over to Ireland. Then, up to Scotland. The Celts were farmers, and makers of useful pottery. They weaved warm colorful sweaters for their families from their sheep. They were a practical people much like my relatives have always been.

The Celts history is being repeated in my own genealogical history. Oh, we're no longer fighting Saxons over grazing lands. But, much of the Celtic way of life still lingers on through me and my relatives' blood lines. Especially with gardening by the signs, and living the simple life. But, most of all in their story-telling tradition.

I'm carrying on the tradition of story-telling in "Living The American Dream." In writing my book I've woven together generational stories of my extended family. Some stories told to me, some I experienced first-hand.

My older relatives vision of the American Dream included plenty of hard work. Their vision is in part how I got to where I'm at. I'm thankful but, arriving at this place in time came about by traveling some "rough roads." On a personal level, and "painting with a broader stroke" on life's canvas as well.

In writing this book I started with an old story I had written about a year ago. I write because it's something I enjoy doing, and it's a cathartic exercise for me as well. So, for reasons unknown to me, I picked this story up again in the middle of this past summer (2016). I began writing with a new vision of what I wanted to say about my parents living their "American Dream." I decided to finish it this time.

This story is about their entrepreneurial success. They set a great example to their five children with their accomplishment. We're all blessed to know in a personal way a couple who started out in their marriage as being low income. But, over time they completely changed their circumstances.

They weren't the likeliest couple to reach the "American Dream." But, through hard work, ambition, and determination they created a successful business.

It's also, a memoir of my parents and their complex multi-layer marriage. A marriage that lasted more than five decades. But, because it took unnecessary twists and turns, it eventually fell apart.

Despite many obstacles though, they did build a successful souvenir import business. Dad named it, Cherokee Sales, Inc. It's located in the community of Whittier, NC. About ten miles from where I live. (Dad is currently closing it down, but it's still open for business.)

Sandwiched in the middle of their story are smaller stories. Stories about the rough "side roads" our lives have taken. Even so, I've been fair and honoring to all I've mentioned.

It's also a story about how my grandparents pulled things together during the Depression. None of them were wealthy. Few even finished school. My maternal grandfather, Dewey Lloyd orphaned at three years old. Even with that my grandfather worked hard, and lived his own "American Dream."

There was a "struggle in their journey" to be sure. But, isn't that the way we still live? Oh, we face different work hardships, but human nature hasn't changed much at all.

In writing this book I've realized I share a generational legacy of strong-willed people. Also, a people who chose to live by their Christian values. It's those important beliefs that have and continue to guide much of my large extended family.

The ethos of human nature to do good rather than harm has won the day throughout my family's generations. And continues to do so. On Facebook, I've noticed how many of my relatives and myself thank God for even the daily things.

I hope you will enjoy reading my book. I hope you will feel inspired to achieve your own "American Dream," if you are not currently doing so. We all have a little bit different idea of what "Living the American Dream" includes. For the most part though, it is possible for each of us to reach our own "American Dream."

My book includes Biblical references where I felt it appropriate to add them. I've used the New Living Translation throughout. Practicing a belief in God has played a dominant role through the generations on both sides of my family. That includes me, also. It wouldn't have been right for me to not include that in my writing.

After reading this story you're welcome to "drop me a line" in my email, or on my Facebook page. I'd like to know how you have or are achieving your own "American Dream."

Sincerely,

Patricia "Trish" Jordan
myjourneyintohealing@gmail.com

CONTENTS

SECTION 1

UP TO AND INCLUDING THE DEPRESSION YEARS

"Wisdom is more valuable than gold..."
—Job 28:17b

LIVING THE AMERICAN DREAM

Many yearn to live the American Dream. The Dream that includes different types of higher education, and near limitless economic opportunities. Home ownership, and countless consumer choices are also included. Some would even add freedom of religion to that list. Of course, not everyone in America who tries to reach "The American Dream" makes it.

Living the American Dream is not all that elusive nor is it selective in any way. The path to achieve it is not an exact one, though. It seems to be a mix of toil, tears, and hardship to be sure. But, it's also a path that has rewards scattered throughout it. Each new reward more treasured than the last one. Hope in a brighter future spurs each one of us on to reach our own personal American Dream.

In an odd mix of planned and un-planned events, many of my older relatives did live their American Dream. Their "un-plans" included plenty of hardship and sacrifice. But, because most of them were "self-starters," they rose from their negative situations. For the most part they made wise choices. They believed that God is in control. And they never ceased at making their tomorrows better than their yesterdays. They made their days count instead of counting their days.

None of my relatives came from privileged or wealthy backgrounds. They reached their goals through their own self-initiative, hard work, and determination. My grandparents raised their children during the Depression. My parents' generation became adults when WWII was raging both in the Pacific and in Europe. Everyone got involved with winning the war back then.

After the men came home they married, became parents, and went to work at everyday jobs. I'm not sure any of them set out to achieve the American Dream in their earlier adult years. I think they felt like they were living it by surviving all they had been through.

MY GRANDPARENTS, THE LLOYDS

My maternal Grandparents, Dewey and Myrtle Lloyd 1920

My maternal grandpa, Dewey Lloyd was born in 1898 in a rural community in western NC. He entered this world by a mid-wife delivering him. He was the oldest of the only two children his mother gave birth to. She died in childbirth with her second child, a boy also. She never married.

My Grandpa's father rejected his illegitimate son. So my grandpa, as a child went from home to home. The 1910 Census shows 12-year-old Dewey Lloyd living with 63-year-old Louize Lloyd. Two of her adult unmarried children also lived with her. I don't know what her exact relationship was, but perhaps she was a great Aunt. I do know that grandpa went by his father's surname.

As a teenager, Grandpa was living in North Georgia on an uncle's farm. By 1915 he enrolled at the Berry Boys Industrial School in Rome, Georgia. Now it's called Berry College. I called Berry's Archive Department to verify that he had enrolled there. They confirmed it from their attendance records from that era. They also informed me that he left there in 1916, not graduating.

In 1917 he joined the Navy during WWI. Then, he married my granny, Myrtle Johnson in 1921. Granny was a farm girl from the rural community of Ogreeta (o greet ah), which is near Murphy, NC. They both grew up about 20 miles or so from each other in the foothills of the Blue Ridge mountains.

By 1925 my two uncles, Jacob (aka J. D.) and Jack were born. Grandpa, was in the Navy at that time. But, he was too far from his young family so he left the Navy. He then went to Ballinger, Texas, and sent for my granny and their two sons to join him. Even in my childhood, Granny talked about that long train ride. She had two rambunctious toddler boys to keep up with.

During the few years they lived there, they added two girls to their family. Their oldest girl's name was June, who became my mother. Mom was born May 17, 1926. They named the youngest girl Mary Jo (aka Jo). She was born November 24, 1927. The girls were always close to each other.

Grandpa found work in a cotton gin in Ballinger. While at work one day he fell from a platform. In falling he cracked his skull on some machinery. He got rushed to the hospital. Someone took my granny to the hospital. The surgeon informed her that he needed to put a metal plate over the crack in grandpa's skull. He told her that grandpa might not survive the operation. As a matter of fact, it was more likely that he might die than live. If ever there was a time to "pray up a miracle" it was then!

Granny had married in her late teens, and had never gone beyond the eighth grade. Prior to moving to Texas she had never lived farther than five or so miles from her large extended family. Now, she was more than a thousand miles from her childhood home in the Smokey Mountains. And she and Grandpa had four young children by the time this serious accident happened.

If not before then, she found out what she was "made of" that day. Pulling her emotions together, she gave permission for the doctor to try and save him. God granted them a miracle. My grandpa walked out of that hospital and he was in his right mind! Not long after that they caught the train back to Western North Carolina.

After surviving that near-death experience, their American Dream included living close to family. During Granny's childhood family members made sure everyone was being cared for. And they carried that tradition on to the next generation. Granny was happiest when she lived near most of her siblings.

The plate the surgeon put in grandpa's head, had in time, caused him to have seizures and black out spells. This limited his employment opportunities, to be sure. But, he never collected any type of disability. I doubt there was such an idea back then.

BUILDING A LEGACY

The Johnson siblings (not pictured are Oscar and Ed). James
Pearl is in center, and my granny is far right on backrow. 1915

All my granny's relatives, the Johnsons lived in the rural
community of Ogreeta. They farmed hundreds of acres of
"bottom land," near Hiwassee Lake in Cherokee County.
They were carpenters by trade. They built their community with
sweat and muscle. But, also with courage, honesty, and determination.
They were building a legacy. A legacy that their descendants are still
"pouring over."

They were a close knit clan that kept up with one another. Even my
mother and her siblings knew most of their cousins on the Johnson
side. Thanks to social media I keep up with my first cousins on both
sides of my family.

All us seventeen grandchildren called my mother's mother

"Granny." But her given name was Myrtle Josephine. She was born in 1903 had been the eighth child in a family of 12 Johnson children. One of the children had died in infancy.

Her parents were John Jacob "Jake" and Sarah Montgomery Johnson. Jake had died in the 1918 influenza epidemic in his fifties. This left about five children still at home that were in their teens or younger. Also, one of the older married daughters had died that year. Her name was Lula, and she left behind five young children.

Jake and Sarah's oldest son, James Pearl Johnson was born in 1891. Everyone called him "Pearl." With the death of his father, Pearl became head of the Johnson clan. He took care of the family thereafter. He was twenty-seven years old and not married by then.

Great Uncle Pearl was tall, lean, and had jet black straight hair. With his tawny skin coloring he "showed" the Cherokee blood that runs through the Johnson clan. Pearl had farmed on family land all his life.

When Uncle Pearl was 46 he and his second wife had my second cousin, John Jacob "Jake" Johnson. I met Uncle Pearl once in my early school years at the old Johnson family home. And I knew Jake throughout my childhood. Today, I keep in touch with Jakes's son, my third cousin John David Johnson.

In my childhood my mother told us five kids about her childhood. She told us about how all the Johnsons came together in the fall to slaughter pigs. Everyone carried home plenty of pork for curing.

When it was time to make syrup the whole clan came together for the days-long event. The men and boys cut and crushed the cane, letting the "juice" run down a chute into a large pot. Then, the women and girls spent hours "skimming" the impurities out. All the while keeping the full pot boiling down. When it was all done, everyone had jars of cane, and sorghum molasses syrup. Molasses was often used in many home remedies.

My mother remembered Grandpa had bartered for a radio by doing some painting for someone. After that, Saturday nights were for listening to The Grand Old Opry from Nashville, TN. Lots of family members showed up to pop popcorn in the fireplace and listen to the radio.

My dad once told us children that a family gettogether with the Johnson clan always included a big meal. To make sure there would be enough tables for the food the men would take the doors off the hinges. Then, they would place the doors on saw horses in the kitchen. If it were nice they set up outside. Every door and counter top was laden with food "fresh from the garden" or canned there in the home.

"Jake" Johnson donated some of his farm land for building a community church and a school house in Ogreeta. Their American Dream included a place to practice their belief in God. They were also, patriotic and served in the military. They worked at strengthening the family ties that bind.

A FATHER REJECTS HIS SON

My grandpa's father admitted to being his father. That was an undeniable fact. Everyone always said Grandpa looked just like his dad. Still, his father disowned his son (my grandpa), all through his childhood. A few years after my grandpa was born his father, had married a local woman. They had two sons a few years younger than my grandpa.

I was always told that grandpa's father and his wife never had anything to do with him. He was never welcomed in their family home. That must've been tough on Grandpa growing up in that small rural community.

Grandpa's father operated the only store in that rural community in western NC. I'm sure my grandpa walked by his dad's store many times a week going to school. Maybe he even went to that store on errands. The main crossroads is where most old country stores located. The communities only school usually was close by, as well.

I'm sure his father's rejection of grandpa hurt him. My mother always said that he took after the Lloyds in all his features. I don't know if she included his short "fuse" of a temper in that description. But, I know she meant him having a deep set of piercing blue eyes, fair skin, and blond hair. He was a small man with an angular lithe frame. Lloyd is Welsh (Celtic), but grandpa's features may have marked him of being more Scottish in origin.

My grandpa grew up with a Christian influence around him. He held onto his Christian faith all his life. He kept his Bible by his porch swing on a small table, along with his wire rimmed glasses. Grandpa attended a white clapboard church near their house. Granny, for some reason never seemed to like that church, so she almost never attended there.

My Aunt Jo told me about meeting grandpa's maternal half-brother during the late 1930's. She told me they were all sitting on the porch, hoping to catch a summer breeze on their farm near Murphy. That's when a nice car drove up in the yard, and a well-dressed man and his wife got out. The man introduced himself as grandpa's half-brother. It caught them all off guard. But, grandpa had always heard he had a brother by his mother. They hadn't seen each other though, since grandpa's early childhood.

Grandpa was only three when his mother died giving birth to his brother. Both boys were immediately given to separate families. When they met again, his brother said that he had taken the name of his new parents. He grew up and became a minister in a close by state.

"SHOULDER TO THE WHEEL"

All four of my grandparents had a strong work ethic. That's what carried that generation through the decade known as The Great Depression. It was that generation that probably coined the phrase "Put your shoulder to the wheel." It means to give it your best, give it your all.

My Grandpa and Granny Lloyd always farmed. They both were extremely hard workers, not given to living by the "whim of their emotions." In the 1930's they were share croppers.

But, the Great Depression made it possible for Grandpa to earn a paycheck again. He worked for the WPA[1] during those years. Men drilled holes in solid walls of granite and then packed the holes with dynamite. After the explosion men guiding mule teams cleared and shaped the roads.

The men traveled all over the Great Smokey Mountains doing this. And in fact, all over America building roads. Groups of men climbed into the back of trucks or buses and traveled dusty rutted roads. They travel to the community that was farthest from the main road. Then, they worked their way to the main roads. New roads meant (and still do mean) being closer to services and better healthcare.

The men also, built schools for their communities. In my seventh and eighth grade years I attended a WPA built school. The main section made from river rock. An "old timer" once told me that they used a mule team and a pulley for lifting and placing each rock in its place. A workable transom window was above every door.

---

[1] Works Progress Administration

This program was a national program that put men back into the workforce along with the CCC[2] program. With the WPA paychecks my grandpa drew he was able to buy about 15 acres that included a small house.

My grandparent's American Dream included patriotism. When WWII started they rented out their farmhouse and moved to Panama City, Florida. They worked in the Naval shipyard there. Their two sons, J. D. and Jack had already joined the Navy by then. Working there kept my granny busier than farming did, which was good. She was very worried about having both sons in the Navy at the same time.

My mother and Aunt Jo stayed behind so they could finish high school together. So, they moved in with relatives in Murphy. They had one more year of high school left. They were a year and a half apart and always did a lot together back then. Even when my mom was six years old she wouldn't start school until Aunt Jo could go to school to.

My mother told us that she was a member of The Beta Club her senior year. That made her an Honor grad of Murphy High School of 1944. Her parents drove up from Florida to see that proud moment in my mother, and Aunt Jo's life. Not long after graduation the four of them went back to Panama City, FL.

Not long after arriving in Florida, Mom went to work at the shipyard. She had just turned eighteen. Aunt Jo didn't get hired right off because she was seventeen. High school only went to the eleventh grade back then. She was too young to work at the "yard" by a few months. Still, there was plenty of work available in town, and they all stayed busy. When Aunt Jo turned eighteen, she worked in the shipyard, also. Both girls became gun turret welders because of their small frame and agility.

Mom was a pretty woman with a beautiful smile that revealed straight white teeth. She had thick wavy auburn hair and a deep set of piercing blue eyes. She always "freckled" when being in the sun.

---

[2] Civilian Conservation Corps

Aunt Jo is a blond, also with a deep set of piercing blue eyes. She never freckled like mom did. Other than that, both could pass for fraternal twins at any stage of their lives.

When the war was over in 1945 all four of them moved back home to Murphy. After that Mom and Aunt Jo rode the bus to Knoxville, TN. They finally could realize their dream of attending the Knoxville Business School.

They shared a small apartment near the old Market Square shopping district. They walked everywhere they could saving their bus fare for rainy days. They only had part-time jobs for that year. Both learned to "stretch" their pennies back then. And that was the way they have lived all their lives.

MY PATERNAL GRANDPARENTS, THE BELLS

My dad, M. G. Bell had a somewhat different childhood experience than my mother. His parents were Clyde C. and Etta (Jones) Bell. Clyde born 1888 in Knoxville, TN. Etta or Grandma as we called her, born in 1901. She also grew up in Knoxville.

They modeled the importance of hard work and Christian values to their four children. They were blue collar people who never owned a home. They lived in an apartment close to Knoxville's old Market Square. On Sundays, all the family walked to the nearest protestant church.

My grandfather, Clyde worked at the Knoxville Railyard as a conductor. He died of a massive heart attack when my dad was almost fourteen. That had such an impact on my dad that he never finished school. He became a "handful" for my grandmother. Not long after dropping out of school, Dad "rode the rails."

When WWII started, my dad came back to Knoxville and joined the Marine Corps. For two years, he stationed at Newfoundland, Canada. While there he obtained his GED. After his discharge, he went back to Knoxville.

My grandmother, Etta became a widow in 1936. It was the height of the Great Depression. Grandma still having three of her four children at home, went to work in the school cafeteria. Grandmother never owned a house, but did live in nice apartments throughout her life. Both she and Clyde taught their children honesty, Godliness, and personal integrity.

Grandma Bell experienced many hardships in her life. Her mother had died giving birth to my grandma. Her father immediately gave her over to a nearby family to raise. My grandmother always called her adoptive mother, Mother White. But, my grandmother's maiden name always was Jones.

Grandma widowed three times altogether. Despite of her hardships though, she saw all four of her children succeed in their chosen careers. And that all four had settled down after WWII to enjoy happy marriages. For all the years, I knew her she seemed content and at peace with life. Her American Dream realized.

THE JOY OF LIVING IN A
SMALL TOWN

My grandparents, 1950's

Y maternal Grandparents, the Lloyds lived a simple life in Murphy. It's always been a small town, located in the foothills of Western North Carolina. They raised their four children on their farm right outside town.

During the Great Depression, they took in older relatives that helped with farming. On Sundays, they went to the closest church that preached Calvinism. Their values centered around family ties, a strong belief in God, and a stronger belief in hard work.

Grandpa never had a license, but did own an old car during my mother's childhood. He rarely drove anywhere though, because of his seizures and blackout spells. Mom told us about riding in a horse drawn wagon during the 1930's. And it didn't matter whether it was raining, snowing, or the sun was shining. In the 1940's, while they lived in Florida, he bought a convertible. He drove it around for only a few years, though.

After WWII, my grandparents lived in the one-story rambling farm house by themselves. Not long after coming back from FL in 1945, they had enough money to have an indoor bathroom added. This increased the size of the kitchen and dining area quite a bit. But, they still got their water from an artesian well even in my early childhood.

Murphy had spread closer to them so they walked into town on shopping days. My grandpa would stand in front of the Rexall Drug store and talk with many of the older men. Granny went into most all the stores to browse. Then, they had their groceries delivered to the back door at about the same time they had walked back home. Later when the A&P built a store a little farther out they took a taxi there and back.

Granny and grandpa always had a large garden. When the produce started coming in Granny began canning, and pickling. She made kraut in the fall. In my childhood, she owned a freezer, but still canned a lot to. I remember her putting green beans on long strings. Then, she tied the strings onto a pole on her screened in back porch and left them there. Granny called these dried green beans "Leather Britches." When she wanted them for supper she put them in pot of boiling water for about half an hour.

She also, always had a yard full of beautiful flowers and bushes. The largest Hydrangeas I've ever seen grew along the driveway. A huge Weeping Willow tree stood at the opposite end of their yard. It was always pleasant to be there, whether we were indoors or outside.

SECTION II

WW II AND AFTERWARDS

Uncle J. D. Lloyd is far right, front row. He was a
mechanic on an Amphibious plane during WWII

FREEDOM IS NEVER FREE

L et us never think that freedom is free. Freedom is costly. The freedom we enjoy comes with the sacrifice of someone else's blood, sweat, and tears. Some have paid and some will pay the ultimate price of giving up their lives for our freedom. Their bravery testifies of their commitment to patriotism. Let freedom ring, but know that it always comes with a price someone must pay.

My maternal grandfather enlisted in the Navy during WWI. He sailed the coastal waters of France on a frigate. Several years ago, I got a copy of his military record. My dad and my uncles served in the military during WWII. To me they are all wartime heroes.

My Uncle J. D. and his younger brother, Uncle Jack Lloyd served in the Navy. Uncle J. D. went to Brazil and worked on amphibious planes. These planes were for search and rescue missions. But, they also took supplies to ships. Uncle Jack assigned to a tanker that sailed the Atlantic Ocean.

To my knowledge, my Uncle Jack Lloyd was my only relative who experienced action during WWII. My brother Gene told me that Uncle Jack's tanker got torpedoed out in the middle of the ocean. That ripped a huge hole in the ship's side!

In a flash, life on board went from calm and routine to total chaos. I'm sure shock seized many men. But, my Uncle Jack kept his wits about him and became a hero. He helped many men, including himself get safely into life rafts. I'm sure these men were grateful beyond words for the heroism he showed that day.

My Uncle Jack nor any of my other uncles, for that matter, talked about their WWII experiences. My dad only told us that he served his

Marine enlistment at Newfoundland, Canada. That base happened to be where planes full of wounded and war shocked men landed first. Then, they went on to military hospitals in the states.

For those of us who have never experienced war it is hard to imagined what our service men and women go through. I'm sure it's difficult to let go of the past traumatic events that they've seen and experienced.

We all must embrace the future, though. It comes to us with each new day. The more positive mindset we have the better off we will be. Of course, that's easier said than done. Reaching the American Dream is possible because of those who serve in our military.

It's important that we show our gratitude to all those that keep America protected. That also, includes our police force that protects our communities. Each of them answer the call to lay down their lives for us. That's a calling that is not for everyone.

I served in the USAF in 1976-1980. I'm proud of being a veteran. My assignment was in Germany. I received a Good Conduct Medal while stationed there. I enjoyed my time there, and went on a couple of MWR[3] tours to beautiful places.

By 1978 I had married Jeff, stationed at the same air base. By 1980 we had our first baby so I decided one enlistment was enough for me. I received an Honorable Discharge at the end of my enlistment.

---

[3] Morale, Welfare, Recreation

Uncle Jack Lloyd, after his enlistment
from the Navy in WWII.

AFTER WWII, AMERICA EXPERIENCED PEACE AND PROSPERITY

The Lloyds

My Aunt Jo, Aunt Mae, and Aunt Barbara. Dad and Mom are on bumper.

B oth of my mother's brothers returned home after the war in perfect physical health. Uncle J. D. came back to visit with his new bride, my Aunt Barbara. Uncle Jack came back and married his hometown girlfriend, my Aunt Mae.

Both of my uncles had a deep set of blue eyes, like their dad. Both had thick wavy hair, J.D. had jet black hair and Jack was a "strawberry" blond. Both men were taller and bigger than their parents. Only my granny put on a bit more weight in her "middle years." Otherwise, like grandpa, none of their kids could keep weight on.

Uncle J. D. and Aunt Barbara lived in Elizabeth City, NC. They had three children, Ken, Donnalene, and Cindy. He became a CPO[4] in the Naval Reserves and made GS 12 as a mechanic at the Coast Guard Base near Elizabeth City. Ken has also achieved CPO in the Navy.

Uncle Jack and Aunt Mae had six children, Cathy, Terry, Jack Jr, Gwen, Peggy, and Steve. He was a butcher in a meat packing house in Asheville, NC, and my Aunt Mae was a waitress at the old Buck's diner on Tunnel Road. Later they moved to central Florida. After they became "empty nesters" they moved back to Murphy.

Aunt Jo met her future husband, Charles Shinlever at Walgreens. They both worked there part-time. He was smitten by the petite, blond cashier with the deep set blue eyes. They married and settled down in Knoxville. That's where they raised their three daughters, Teresa, Debbie, and Jolene.

Aunt Jo has shaped a loving, home-life for her family. And, she still lives in the house they bought in the 1950's. Like her mother, Aunt Jo has always gardened but, on a much smaller scale. She has also planted beautiful flowering plants all around their house. Visiting her is like walking through a miniature botanical garden. She has also enjoyed traveling to visit with her grandchildren and great-grandchildren. They have "spread their wings" to live way beyond Knoxville.

Upon his discharge from the Navy, Uncle Charles enrolled at the University of Tennessee. After graduating UT, he became a high school physics teacher. He taught for thirty-nine years, altogether. Thirty-eight of those years at Fulton High School in Knoxville.

Several of his students became doctors at the UT Medical Center. When Uncle Charles needed a pacemaker, he ran into several of them there. Many more of his students traveled the world doing great things.

---

[4] Chief Petty Officer ((highest enlisted rank in the navy)

Yet, he was the kind of father that would stay up late on a Friday night to play board games with his daughters. Their American Dream included their children having a good education. All three graduated UT with education degrees.

Uncle Charles, also did something that has always impressed me. He dug out a full-size basement under their house. Aunt Jo told me that he had one of their girls wait outside the crawl space with a wagon. When he filled the wagon up with dirt then one of their girls would dump it in the lower part of their backyard.

To enter the basement, he got the Carpentry Shop students and teacher to build a "bump out" to the living room wall. Then, they went inside and took the living room outside wall out. This gave their living room about a four-foot alcove addition, with a door to the basement. Their house has a sloping backyard. He added a basement window to the block, and the alcove had the original window put back in.

Later Uncle Charles added a den. Once again, he worked with the Carpentry Shop teacher and his students to build the outside of it. Uncle Charles and Aunt Jo finished the interior with "knotty pine" paneling. Both sections are still beautiful, seamless additions.

THE BELL'S

My dad's oldest brother, Uncle Harold had already joined the Navy during WWII. After his discharge, he married my Aunt Libby and they had five children: Jerry, Lyn, Jewel, Linda, and Cathy. Plus, his son, Victor "Buddy" from his first marriage. He worked as a draftsman for the TVA[55.] Uncle Harold had enormous musical talent. He played several instruments well. One instrument he played the best was the steel guitar. He played that in local Country Music bands.

Dad's sister, Dorothy married Buddy Crisp and they had two daughters. Uncle Buddy brought the first chain grocery store to Knoxville, a Piggly Wiggly. Aunt "Dot," was a long-time secretary at Scruggs Supply Co. As I heard it, she was more in charge at work than the boss! It took a while, but she became the office manager.

My dad's youngest brother Wayne Bell, enlisted in the Marine

Grandma Bell with Dad, and two friends.

---

[5] Tennessee Valley Association

Corp during the 1950's. After his discharge, he returned to Knoxville and married my Aunt Mary. They have two sons, Danny and Mark.

When Uncle Wayne returned to Knoxville he became a Knoxville Police Officer. He has been on the police force for over fifty-one years. He was the "Eye in the Sky" for Knoxville highways for several years. He, also has held various positions in the TN Shriners organization.

Mom's theater employee pass

WHEN MY PARENTS MET, AND FELL IN LOVE WITH EACH OTHER

A worthy wife is a crown for her husband,
(Proverbs 12:4a)

My parents met in Knoxville after dad came home from WWII. Mom and Aunt Jo were already attending the Knoxville Business School at that time. Mom had an after-school job selling tickets for the movies.

Well, my dad liked going to the movies after work. The movie theater was within walking distance of where he lived, so he went often. One evening, he noticed the new ticket seller. She was a pretty brunet who had a beautiful smile. Dad took an immediate interest in her. Of course, that petite brunet was my future mother.

After meeting mom, dad going to the movies also meant talking to her on her break. They soon realized they were a good "match" for each other.

In May of 1946 my parents married. Mom had graduated the business school by then. Afterwards, they moved to Murphy. Mom always enjoyed living in a small town, and wanted to be near her parents.

My mother's 1944 high school graduation picture, Murphy, NC.

SMALL BEGINNINGS DO ADD UP

Do not despise these small beginnings...
—Zech. 4:10a

My dad went through several jobs while they lived in Murphy. My mother though, kept a steady job as a secretary for the only dentist in town. During the seven or so years they lived there all five of us were born. My brother Gene was born March 1947; Carol is next born March 1948. Deena's born in August 1949, David's born in December 1950. I'm the youngest one born May 1952. It was a busy time for my parents. It's a good thing that my grandparents lived close by and babysat us.

David was born underweight and sickly. Our mom spent a whole year taking him to the only pediatrician in the local area. There was one west of Asheville, NC. His practice located here in Sylva. This meant her and David getting on a Trailways or Greyhound bus once a week in Murphy. They then, traveled about fifty miles for David's checkup. Then they took the bus all the way back to Murphy. Everything done in one long day.

My parents told us how poor they were back in those days. A local church took notice of my parents with five small children to feed. Church members visited us with food baskets. Of course, I don't remember any of that. But, my parents never forgot that show of Christian love and kindness from strangers.

After a few years, dad got a snack route with Tom's Peanuts. He loved being out on the road meeting store owners. He took in fresh snacks, arranged the rack. He asked if he could place his rack in a better location. Dad knew that buying snack food is an impulse decision. So, the closer to the cash register he could get his display the better.

That was his first sales job. And getting that route sales job "launched" him into a sales career. Years later his sales talent made him and my mother millionaires! But, I'm getting ahead of myself.

"SELF-STARTERS" CHANGE
THEIR LIFE'S DIRECTION

It pays to be a "self-starter" in reaching the American Dream. That phrase describes my parents to a "T." Neither of my parents were "couch potatoes." They were energetic all through much of their lives. My dad is 92, and still goes to the warehouse every day. He is selling off the remaining stock himself, using a small workforce.

About 1956 my parents left Murphy. They moved us about 70 miles east to the city of Asheville, NC. We moved around in West Asheville. But,we finally settled down in a rented house right outside of Asheville late in the year of 1958. We lived out in the country and had a big yard, in the Fairview community. Mom was happy so she put her foot down on any more moving. We lived there long enough for me to go from the first grade to the end of my sixth grade.

During the years, we lived in Fairview, my older sister Carol took over getting us five ready for the school bus. During the summers, she took charge of us while our parents were at work. Year around, for five days a week Carol made sure we had a hot breakfast every morning.

Carol turned twelve a few months after we moved there. It was a lot of responsibility for a preteen to take on. But, I don't remember anything catastrophic happening during those years either. We five were never late for school, and enjoyed our summer months off living way out in the country.

My dad sold restaurant equipment throughout the region. He left the house early and rarely came in until we had already eaten supper.

My mom worked at a small factory in Fairview, and kept our home life on a steady routine.

By the time mom arrived home from work Carol and Deena had some of our supper started. Then, Mom finished cooking a delicious hot meal for us every night. We're still thankful for her tireless efforts. Because of mom our family life had developed into a good routine of work or school during the weekdays. Saturdays were for grocery shopping. On Sundays, we attended church at Fairview Baptist. Mom loved the mountains. So, on occasion, we skipped church to picnic. Sometimes we went to Craggy Gardens or the Pink Beds in the Pisgah National Forest.

My mother had a strong controlling personality. I wouldn't describe her as personal, but she was friendly and caring. Mom was honest, had a strong work ethic, and a straightforward way of talking. Everyone respected my mother. Her qualities helped her get promotions at work.

Mom was more outward in her care for us, than dad. She cared about her family as much as anyone could. She could be patient at times, but she always was firm in her discipline. Mom didn't want us five growing up to be a "bunch of whiners." She made us take responsibility for our actions.

Mom wasn't a "hugger" but, she did show her love for us by what she did for us. I'm sure we misunderstood her love at times. Mom didn't "hand out" her approval with the chores we did. But, still we five have always loved and respected our Mother.

Mom trained my sisters and I in the "art" of keeping a meticulous house. It was quite a challenge with seven people plus a dog all crammed into a 1000 sq. ft. house. But, she and we girls did chores. We girls washed the daily laundry and hung it out. As I've said, we never received a reward, but knew it had better get done before Mom got home. She expected a lot from us girls and we tried to never disappoint her.

Sometimes, in my childhood Dad would play board games with us kids. He always made sure we went on a yearly vacation when mom got her week off. All-in-all though, my dad "parented from a distance." He wasn't much involved in our daily routine. It often seemed to me that Mom was our only parent.

To me Dad's always been self-focused. His routine has always included eating a late supper, then playing his organ. In my childhood, after Dad had his supper, he then "ran" us kids off to take baths and go to bed. That's when he sat at his organ and spent an hour or so playing it.

Dad "saddled" mom down with a lot of the day-to-day parenting. He solved our sibling arguing by acting with swiftness and harshness. The guilty and the innocent got the same treatment. Why did he whip us girls when our brothers created conflict? I don't know.

OVERCOMING STUTTERING

L-R: Carol, Deena, me, David, Gene. Mid-1950's

When I was a young child I stuttered. Almost no one understood what I was trying to say. My parents found it difficult hearing me stutter. So, both directed me to communicate my needs or wants to my two older sisters. It was Carol or Deena who were more "in tune" to me back then. I thank God for both of my sisters taking care of me the way they did in my childhood. We three are still close today.

In my first-grade year, we moved from busy West Asheville to the rural community of Fairview. We lived there for six years. During those years, my siblings and I attended the small Fairview Elementary School. The school went from the first to the eighth grade.

Moving there worked to my favor. When I entered the third-grade I had Mrs. Allison for a teacher. She was a kind older teacher who took an immediate interest in helping me with my speech. I was shy and usually let my sisters do the talking for me.

Mrs. Allison proved to be a true "Godsend" for me. Through her many years of teaching she had become a wise and insightful teacher. In fact, she was so insightful that she stopped me from stuttering. Perhaps, she considered my future. Realizing that sooner or later I needed to start doing my own talking. So, why not start then.

I don't recall ever going to a speech teacher. I doubt Fairview, like many rural schools back in the early sixties had a speech therapist.

It did take Mrs. Allison all that school year to get me to slow down my speech pattern. I had to pronounce each word during class reading time. It was a challenge to get me to speak up during class time in general. I hated reading out loud and rarely raised my hand.

Avoidance didn't work with her, though. During reading time, I remember her resting one of her hands across my back. Then she would point to each word that I was to read out loud with her other hand.

I had to sound out each word while she coaxed me along using calming words of assurance. Her common-sense approach worked. I don't recall that I ever stuttered after that year. I was still bashful for years afterwards about answering questions or reading aloud. It took a long time for me to overcome my shyness.

After that school year, I had my tonsils taken out because I had strep throat a lot. When I got home from surgery my parents had a blue girls bike waiting for me. That was exciting, but it didn't compare to a special visitor I had a few days after I got home. My favorite teacher, Mrs. Allison had stopped by to check on me and listen to me read aloud.

"THINKING OUTSIDE THE BOX"

My dad has always been an "out of the box" thinker. This is an important characteristic to have in becoming a successful entrepreneur. Risk taking is a part of that, but needs to be well thought out. If taking risks could be place on a scale the counter balance needs to always be gain-loss.

My mother was not a risk taker at all. She provided the counter-balance to many of my dad's ideas. Mom was much like the Celtics of old. They lived their days by doing practical and useful things. All their family benefited from their practicableness, like we did in my childhood.

Mom was not only practical throughout her life. She saw things as they were. Not as we hope for them to be. She thought in the day-to-day realm. That life happens in minutes, hours, and days. Then the days become a pattern of our individual lives. That type of vision is its own talent.

She would always weigh the "pros and cons" of dad's ideas. Moving five school age children around to "chase after dreams" wasn't her "cup of tea." She, like most of us women, loved living with a sense of security. Mom was routine about the order of things, as well. But, her routine is where us kids found our security. We could almost set our Timex (if we'd had one) by our mom's routine.

Still, they knew change was necessary if they were to reach something better than what they had. Renting a cinderblock house wasn't bringing them the change they both sought after.

What they did realize was that their work careers had "boxed" them in. The harder they worked the more nothing changed in their finances. After six years of steady work their finances hadn't changed. They had no hope of ever owning a house in the foreseeable future.

Change is inevitable. Our goals need to guide the direction of change. How well we accept the outcome often decides the paths we take, afterwards.

SHIFTING THEIR PARADIGM

A "paradigm shift" means to have a complete change of directions. Achieving this almost always means to disrupt a routine that we've grown used to.

Both of my parents realized it's easy to get settled into the "rote" routine of life. But, routine doesn't always bring advancement. Change can bring advancement. My parents desired a change of direction in their lives. This is how they achieved their goals. And, they didn't wait for perfect timing to make those changes either.

Neither Dad or Mom "dithered or dawdled around" when it came to making big decisions. They did come into agreement on most of their ideas. After that, they begin overcoming the obstacles in their way in moving our family of seven. They did what they had to do so they would have better job opportunities. Home ownership being their goal during those years.

MOVING TO THE CHEROKEE INDIAN RESERVATION

I n the spring of 1964 we had moved to the Cherokee Indian Nation (Reservation). Dad and Mom had decided it was time to change our family routine forever. By then, he'd convinced her that she could operate a small souvenir shop. Much like the ones we had seen in the Cherokee Indian Reservation. We had to pass through there on our way to Murphy to visit our grandparents.

Dad had noticed an empty store building on the Cherokee Indian Reservation. It was a small block building that was on US 19 across the Oconoluftee River from Frontier Land.

Mom decided to give dad's idea about operating a souvenir shop a try. They had little to lose. So, in the summer of 1964 she quit her plant job. And we moved about fifty miles west to the Cherokee Indian Reservation. The first year we had the souvenir store, Mom and I ran it seven days a week through the summer months. My older siblings got summer jobs, elsewhere.

We lived behind the store in a used 3-bedroom trailer for three years. By the second year my dad got Mom to manage the Tom Tom Restaurant. Sometimes, that meant her being the cook, sometimes it meant her being a waitress. Mom wore "many hats" during those years.

Operating the restaurant turned out to be stressful. Mom was always loyal to dad, but she had her "breaking points." And one of those "points" turned out to be the Tom Tom. That's with me looking back to what I can remember.

During the two years Mom ran the restaurant my older sister Deena, a teenager at the time, managed the gift shop. I, of course, helped her. After closing the shop in the evening, we often ate supper at the restaurant. That's when Deena helped in waitressing. Sometimes I washed dishes. Mom went home to rest at that time. Dad took over being the cashier, or Carol. She had become a waitress there.

Dad had place an organ in a corner of the restaurant so he could play it whenever possible. He loved entertaining the customers with Lawrence Welk's Champagne music. Many others also enjoyed playing the multi-tier organ as well.

My brothers worked at summer jobs as soon as we moved to the Reservation. David was only about thirteen then. But he worked with Gene at a campground for a couple of summers. We all stayed busy with the tourist trade for about four months a year. During the winter months, our home life seemed to settle back down. We attended Cherokee Baptist Church, at least for a few winters.

During our Christmas break, we camped out in Florida. We traveled all the way to the Seminole Indian Reservation near Fort Lauderdale, FL. I remember us stopping in Atlanta, and eating Krystal hamburgers in the middle of the night. Gene had his license by then so he helped with the driving. We didn't stop for long until we got all the way to the beach.

Of course, all this new activity "shifted" the routine of our home life a lot. But, the routine of home wasn't all that important to my dad. He loved selling so much that he continued to work long hours in sales during this time. In the evenings and weekends, he went to the restaurant to eat his meals.

A STORY WITHIN A STORY

I n writing this book I realized that I've developed two stories. One story is biographical "sketches" of many of my relatives, including myself. The main part being about my parents, though.

My dad has always been a persuasive communicator. But, Mom was not his "yes" person. She stood up to him and said "No" when she needed to. In the early years of their business that wasn't as difficult as it became latter on to do. That "in a nutshell" is one half of what my book is about.

The other story is about the key characteristics my parents had that worked for them. Those characteristics that helped them in becoming successful entrepreneurs. I've tried to include all the "special ingredients." The ones they had and have as individuals and, as a couple. It's those "ingredients" that led them to both reach and to live their American Dream.

I hope you the reader know that I'm not encouraging anyone to become a self-absorb person. That is not my goal and never will be.

I've been honest in describing both of my parents' personalities. It's not possible to separate their personal story from their business story. It's all too intertwined for that to be possible. I'm over any ill-feelings I may have harbored against either of my parents that carried over into my adulthood. I've forgiven and love them both.

WEALTH BUILDING: HAVING A MILLION DOLLAR IDEA

D ad developed what turned out to be a million-dollar idea during the two years mom managed the restaurant. When he ate his meals there he met many of the local craft shop owners who also ate there. They told him how hard it was for them to get a variety of cheap souvenirs to sell in their shops. Listening to them gave Dad the idea of starting a souvenir wholesale business.

Being a good listener has its rewards. Questioning almost always goes with listening. To my dad's credit he has always shown a keen interest in ideas that inspires his creativeness. In listening to the shop owners, he was able to turn his and my mother's business direction around. They went from "retail thinking" to "wholesale selling."

In moving to Cherokee, my parents' goal was not to become millionaire "wealth builders." Not at first, anyway. I never heard either of them use that phrase. What drove them to leave our settled routine in Fairview was the desire for home ownership. In the six years of living in Fairview, the best they could do was to have a small savings account. Any small emergency that happened would drain that account.

Neither of my parents ever had a "get by" attitude about their work efforts. That alone, was a driving force for them to do better. So, after we got "settled in" to a new routine in Cherokee, both of my parents became "awakened." They began to see the money-making possibilities that were available to them. One successful idea led to another. The work was demanding, though.

Many of the business on the Reservation were, and still leased to non-Indians. People come from all over to manage shops, eateries, and entertainment there. My parents only leased the shop and then the restaurant. So, when they quit managing these businesses mom could've been out of a job. But, two years of restaurant work had made her angry and difficult to be with. She was ready for and needed a change.

Closing the restaurant down when they did was good timing on various levels. For one, it saved their marriage. The other was that my parents had time to launch dad's latest idea. This idea turned out to be their true niche. His idea was for them to start a joint enterprise of wholesaling souvenirs to the shop owners. This idea is how they achieved living their American Dream.

SECTION III

★ ★ ★ ★ ★ ★ ★ ★

LIVING THE AMERICAN DREAM

Mom and Dad, early 1970's

TURNING THE AMERICAN DREAM INTO REALITY

I n 1967 my parents acted on dad's new business idea. It was an immediate success. Whole-selling souvenirs is what lead them to living their American Dream. They became "wealth builders" from that point onward.

That year, Mom and Dad closed both the shop and restaurant. They had purchased about four acres in nearby Whittier, and moved our trailer there. Then, they launched their wholesale souvenir business. Dad named it, Cherokee Sales Co. Inc. (CSC Inc.).

Dad was the company's CEO and only salesperson. He started with a backseat full of samples and a few B&W pictures of more samples. He began selling in Cherokee. Then he worked every souvenir shop in the Great Smoky and Blue Ridge Mountains. To my dad's credit he learned early the importance of asking questions. By the time, they launched their business Dad already knew a few wholesale suppliers.

Right after I graduated high school in 1970, mom started traveling with dad. She took charge of the commercial bank account and became CSC's CFO. Dad knew she was better at managing money than he was. There wasn't much of a fight about it back then, nor much to fight over.

When I left in 1971, dad had extended his sales route to include several states. He started accumulating a lot of "quick sale" items. So, they rented old buildings to store it. It was during that time that they hired Gene to help mom pack orders. Then, Gene would deliver the boxes to shop owners in different tourist destinations. He established certain days for deliveries early on. Dad had spread out his regular sales territory to include the edges of three states: North GA, East TN, and WNC.

About 1975 mom and dad had built a beautiful spacious brick home in Whittier, NC. Mom loved that house. She immediately established flower beds full of Zinnias, Marigolds, and so on. On a trip to Murphy she got Gene to dig up roots of some of her parents flowering bushes and added those to her yard. Mom lined the front of their house with flaming red Azaleas. Red was always her favorite color. When she painted her nails, they were bright red.

Mom took over the den and organized their first business office in it. They used the garage for storing some of their growing inventory. As I've stated their business was successful from the start. Shop owners were "hungry" for the new, and wider variety of souvenirs my parents offered.

In the eighties, Dad purchased their second RV. This one was longer than the first one. It was a beautiful deep blue. He had flown to the manufacture to pick it out himself, then drove it back home.

In each RV, he had a carpenter turn the "living room" area into a miniature showroom. In place of a closet and cabinets there were 12" x 12" shelving that pulled out like dresser drawers. Each drawer had samples of Smokey Mountain souvenirs Velcro onto a mat placed in each drawer. Tiny roaring black bears in the bear drawer, coffee cups in a deeper drawer, and so on. He and mom also made similar sample boards that they stored in the luggage compartments.

Buying the RVs enabled mom and dad to work with the shop owners at their shops. Also, since the fall of 1970 they had traveled as far north as Lake Placid, NY. Then, after a rest at home they would travel as far south as Biloxi, MS.

They traveled to the tourist destinations to sell souvenirs to the shop owners. They had samples that fit that region's theme from a supplier on the west coast. They also took time to visit each area as well. Mom loved Hershey, PA most of all. Not only is it quaint, but it always has a good supply of fresh made chocolate available. My mom was a petite size woman who had a big "sweet tooth!"

About this same time, UPS had built a hub in Sylva, about 20 miles from their house. After getting home they, and Gene packed the orders. Then, shipped them via UPS. Having that hub nearby transformed their business. It helped them go from being a regional souvenir supplier to an East Coast supplier. They knew most of the good restaurants on I-95 as well as anybody could.

In 1987 they purchased about six acres of sloping land on US 441 in Whittier. They had a large area bulldozed out for a warehouse and parking. Dad had built a 5000-square foot tan metal building there. Inside he had a showroom for samples, two offices, and one bathroom. In the back, he enclosed a small workroom for heat pressing decals on tee shirts.

They let Gene design the large warehouse stock area with rows of metal shelving. He then, arranged the stock. It all had an order and "flow" to it. Of course, each year the arrangement shifted because of adding or deleting merchandise.

Gene had "squeaked by" in high school. He got drafted not long after graduating in 1965. Then, he received a medical discharge within ninety days. After that he enrolled in our county's new technical school, and took electronics. He excelled in it. This was when they used a slide-rule instead of fancy calculators. All, were amazed at his math abilities. He worked in that field until the mid-seventies.

That's when Mom and Dad hired him to pack orders in the old rented buildings. I guess moving back home appealed to him. Gene was always close to mom. He was living in Murphy, NC at that time. He worked for Litton Industries where his ex-wife worked. Moving back to Whittier, gave him that change he needed.

Mom and Dad hired David as a warehouse worker after they built the warehouse in 1987. He became their delivery person. Both sons received house sites there. The warehouse is located about two miles from the Cherokee Indian Reservation.

Within a few more years, they hired my oldest sister Carol, as a salesperson. They also, hired another salesperson. By then they were "Living the American Dream!"

Before building the warehouse, dad went to Hong Kong. He traveled with a souvenir jewelry supplier from Miami, FL. This man showed dad "the ropes" of how to be his own importer. After that dad, mom, and Gene went there once each year. They caught the wholesale shows and met with several Asian manufacturers. After a few years, they took Carol. By that time, they were traveling to Beijing, China.

TROUBLE IN PARADISE

Even in paradise trouble can be "brewing." It takes adding a few negative ingredients to turn up the heat of anger to make a simmering pot boil over.

My parents traveled the open road together in a plush RV through the first ten years of their business. Then, they started going to China together. Over the years, they had developed many different lines of souvenirs and gift items. This, of course meant them having many different suppliers.

Some of those manufacturers are in Hong Kong. So, they would go there first to checked in with these companies. After that, they went on to Beijing, China. They always went when the major manufacturers in China have their trade shows. That's when all the latest products are on display.

They took Gene, and Carol with them. Gene never sold for CSC. But, he still had a pretty good "feel" for what would sell and not sell on many ideas. Carol and mom chose much of the gift line. And home décor ideas.

On in their marriage my mother didn't always go on these long trips to China. I can only speculate why. Mom and we five have always loved our dad. But, none of us would call him the easiest man to live with by any means.

I would describe my dad as having an enigmatic, but difficult personality. He has never bothered asking. In my childhood, he ordered us to get it done or risk the consequences.

Dad's an average looking man. He's about 5'7, has limp brown hair, brownish eyes, and olive tone skin coloring. But, even in his nineties he still has an aggressive dominating "presence" about him.

Dad's a self-taught organist. He has a great "ear" for music. We always had a two-tier organ in our house in my childhood. He didn't like bothering with the details of parenting. Instead, he came home from work, and ate his supper while watching Walter Cronkite give the news. Then, he would tell us kids to get our bath and go to bed. Then, he turned off the TV and played his organ for an hour or so.

On the most part, dad is a soft tone talker. It's always been rare to hear him talk above medium level. Out in public he's always been "Mister Likeable." Mom always said he's a complex and multi-layer thinker.

Dad's a "lefty." When I went back to college in my forties I took a few psychology courses. I remember reading in one of those books about "left handed-right brain" men. They almost always have aggressive personalities.

"BIG PICTURE" THINKING VS "DETAIL" THINKING

Personality wise, both of my parents were (and are) controllers. This bought on stress since both couldn't be right on everything. My dad is a "big picture" thinker so he's always wanted to control the outcome. My mother thought through every detail. She wanted to control the steps it took to create the "big picture." When they stuck with what they were both good at then things went smooth.

They loved each other and did come together on a lot of good ideas. My mother gifted in "left brain" analytical thinking skills, organized the office. "Paperwork" never has interested dad. He continued selling throughout the regional tourist areas. He handed over all office duties to mom, and also let her do the hiring and firing of the warehouse help. Most of the help usually stayed on for several years, though.

Mom supervised the warehouse office for twenty-five years. During those years, she only had two women to help her in the office at different times. The first one Bobbi Johnson stayed about ten years. The last one, Donna Cannon is a CPA. She took over a lot of the day-to-day grind during the last fifteen years of mom's life.

My sister-in-law Janice (Cooper) Bell did fill in at the office in the beginning. Janice and David met when we entered the seventh grade at Qualla Elementary. They were high school sweethearts. They married about a year after we graduated high school.

David, Janice, and I all went to the new technical school in our county after high school. David wanted to be an accountant. Janice took secretarial courses. I studied drafting. By the end of that year we all three had dropped out of our respective two-year programs.

David and Janice married and moved to Chattanooga, TN. A few years later they moved back to Whittier, and never left. At that time, David worked at a local Ingles Supermarket. They had their two children by about that time.

In a few years of that Janice began nursing training. She is a full-time nurse. But in the early years of CSC Inc. she worked at the warehouse office on her days off. Much later, my husband Jeff did deliveries for CSC Inc. for a few months while he went to CDL school on the weekends. Other relatives have worked there as well.

Another woman who has stayed a long time is Peggy Dehart. She has heat-pressed decals on tee shirts and helped in the warehouse for more than ten years. Of course, there have been a few others who have come and gone.

I worked there for two summers. It wasn't a pleasant experience for me. Most of the time we were all busy. I contributed to the work force as much as anyone else there did. I did janitorial work, stocked shelves, helped Peggy with tee shirts. I became the sales person in the showroom, as well. As it turned out I, also was good at selling. I only sold in the showroom, but it did take a chore off mom's shoulders.

Even with all that I did, the atmosphere at the warehouse was always like a feudal serfdom. Dad was the "vassal." Crossing the moat to enter his kingdom wasn't always a pleasant experience for me. I was always on the "outside looking in." I didn't speak the "village serf speech" at all. I'm not saying others did, I'm only speaking for myself here.

Mom was kind enough, but personal warmth was never her "strong suit." She made excuses for everyone's show of low respect. I wondered out loud why she was enabling dad's poor behavior in their marriage. After that, it was better for me to avoid dad altogether.

Gene was the only bachelor among us five. In his twenties, he married for six months then divorced. He never married again after that. So, the warehouse was an extension of himself, more than it's been to my siblings and myself. I saw it as a job, but did think I would enjoy working for my parents. It proved to be a difficult experience for me, though.

He ruled the inventory placement. If I stocked the boxes parallel instead of perpendicular to the shelf space, he had an anxiety attack. The warehouse had many rows of long, wide metal shelving that was about 15 ft. high.

Gene never accepted "change." Change is inevitable, though. None of us can avoid "change." And "change" is constant. Of course, we all need to "draw a line" on what each of us can tolerate. We can't always keep up with constant change even if we tried to.

My mother, to her credit, stayed as emotional stable as was possible for her. All through my childhood and at the warehouse to she was our "Rock Steady." We'll never know how much emotional stress she went through, because she hid it so well.

My parents with grandson Jacob Long. Early 1980's.

ON A POSITIVE NOTE

O n the positive side of things mom did bring a lot of unity to their workforce. One of her daily "unspoken" tasks was to keep things on a steady emotional keel. Not easy to do when Dad would feel like being unkind or dodge responsibility for a blunder he had made. My dad does have a few un-admirable qualities about him.

Later they hired their bookkeeper, Donna Cannon to run the office. I saw Donna stand up to dad, time and again when I worked there. Dad's aggressive style of communication can come across as brusque. I've never heard my dad give an apology for being harsh with any of us. But, maybe he has, and I don't remember it.

Donna encouraged my very smart mom, in correcting her marriage-business situation. Mom did seek a lawyer's advice in the end. She often "stood up" for mom, as well. Mom could hold her own, but she was in her seventies by this time, too. Mom confided in Donna, and trusted her judgement.

Back to my original thought. Mom did bring unity to the warehouse. One way was in her cooking. She was an excellent cook. Over the weekends mom put together lunch ideas for everyone at the warehouse. She often baked a picnic ham or a turkey breast over the weekend. Then, on Monday she would take a platter of either meat to the kitchenette refrigerator. Everyone could make themselves a thick sandwich. Mom willingly did these things to. Cooking was one of her many talents. Making sure her family and the other workers were well fed brought a lot of joy to her.

Mom kept the kitchenette shelves stocked with cans of soup,

potted meat, cookies, and a fresh loaf of bread. Sometimes they grilled out on Fridays or Mom ordered pizza for everyone. David always got there early and started the coffee brewing.

In the 1980's David and Gene helped form the Qualla Volunteer Fire Department. They took over our old, empty elementary school, and cut bays for the trucks. After a few years, Gene didn't care for the "politics" of it, so he resigned.

David stayed on though, and became Fire Chief. He secured the funds for building the new station. He had it built where our old elementary school had stood. He contacted Moore Metal Buildings and got bids from other builders. Moore got the bid. David also requested and got built a substation about five miles away. He recently retired from being chief. He still loves it though, and shows up for all the meetings.

Our mother instilled within us the importance of volunteering. She taught Sunday School or worked in the nursey at church. Mom, also donated odds-and-ends of outdated souvenirs to the local elementary school.

We girls have volunteered while our children attended school. At present, I volunteer at and stay active in my church. Our American Dream includes volunteering.

FISSURES IN THE FOUNDATION

Fissures in a foundation can cause a magnificent castle to become rubble. Of course, it takes time for this type of destruction to happen. Time is what it takes to ignore foundational problems in any relationship. Even more so in marriage.

Dad has always said what he thinks and doesn't think about what he says. Emotional negative undercurrents can rule his day. My mother became adapt at making excuses for him. Some would say that she "enabled" him to continue in his bad habits, even though it worked to her detriment in doing so.

It's only my opinion, but I believe my dad has an undiagnosed personality disorder. He has always had high positive energy "up swings" then he "bottoms out" in anger. Late in their marriage mom did get Dad to go to a counselor. Mom told me that he sat through one or two sessions, then stomped out the door. That was the end of that.

Accepting the possibility of him having a personality disorder brings me closure. Over his harsh discipline, I experienced as a child. But, both of my parents disciplined harshly.

SAVING GRACE

There were some "saving graces" that dad has never forgotten. One, is that mom loved and believed in dad. That was a difficult thing to do at times, though. When he had caused some damage in their relationship, he would patch things up. Then, mom forgave him and they would move on through life together for at least a while longer.

Dad loved mom in his own odd way. He admired her organizational talents, as well. He is a forgetful "scatter brain." Mom never understood what that term meant. She could remember meeting someone a year earlier and would greet them by name.

They got back into attending Cherokee Baptist on a regular basis, after I had left in 1971. They ceased to work on the weekends by then and had settled into a standard work week routine. Dad played the organ and had become a deacon. Mom volunteered in the nursery. Mom made sure they were tithers with their money.

The other "saving grace" is that dad knows he's lucky that he married mom. He married "up," as the old saying goes. Mom's the one who pulled their finances together. It's one thing to make a lot of money. But, it's a different idea when it comes to knowing where it's all going to.

Dad did make sure both he and mom drove nice cars, though. He has always had a sporty Chrysler coupe convertible. Plus, he's always had a company supplied van. Mom always drove a big beautiful Lincoln sedan.

They owned the warehouse and land privately. Once the warehouse got built, their company leased it to them. They charged

CSC Inc. a yearly lease fee of $36,000. In time mom and dad went to a financial counselor over their different ideas of what to do with the rent. Dad has never been as thrifty as mom had been.

Mom always stayed true to her "roots." She furnished their home comfortably, but not in an expensive fashion. She always "pinched" her pennies, though. Mom drove her car for at least five years or more. They always took her car on big trips so in five or so years it had plenty of miles on it.

The counselor suggested they have two different retirement accounts. That idea worked for both. Doing this solved a lot of "heated" discussions between the two of them.

LOCATION, LOCATION, LOCATION

When my parents built the original warehouse in 1987 they added David, plus the office help. They gave keys to both Gene and David. They let my brothers work there as needed during the winter. Both were always on a straight salary. Mom and dad went to Florida and didn't come back until late February. At least that was the way it worked for a few years.

Their wholesale business built upon selling souvenirs by the dozens. By the 1980's the tourists' centers that sold the souvenirs wasn't staying small anymore. Dad's timing of building the warehouse couldn't have been better. Locating it about two miles from where we had lived since 1967 was convenient, as well.

Whittier is still rural, but near some large tourist areas. Close by is the Eastern Band of the Cherokee Indian Nation Reservation. The "Tribe" began improving their shopping areas around the mid-eighties. Most of the old shops from my childhood torn down, replaced with improved parking and nice shops.

Frontier Land had become a real "ghost town." The Tribe demolished it, and built Harrah's Casino on that land. They added a lot more acreage to the Casino as well.

Island park where US 441 and US 19 split use to be an outcropping of rocks in the middle of the Oconoluftee River. Now it's a beautiful large park where kids of all ages splash and play in the water.

Next on US 441 North is Gatlinburg, TN. It's a large tourist center that's about forty-five miles from the warehouse. In my childhood, we would walk down the main sidewalks there and watch the workers pull and shape taffy. During the eighties, it started growing by "leaps and bounds." Now, Gatlinburg is open all year around with lots to do.

Right after Gatlinburg is Pigeon Forge, TN., which is spreading toward Sevierville, TN. A Tanger Outlet mall took over several acres of farmland between the two towns. Then, some large-scale amusements, and hotels got built nearby. The farmland between the tourist centers and the town began disappearing fast in the 1980's. Dollywood and Splash Country located right outside Pigeon Forge.

CSC, Inc warehouse fire, 2001.

TESTED BY FIRE

"Dear friends, don't be surprised at
the fiery trials you are going through..."
—1Peter 4:17

So far I've mentioned several ways mom demonstrated her commitment to dad and the business. But, there was one big event that was difficult for me to grasp, at least at that time. It happened in the early Spring of 2001.

The warehouse exploded into a ball of fire one cold March morning that year. The reason that it happened did fall on my dad's shoulders. When he built the warehouse, he didn't put heat in the cavernous stock area. When their business was still small Mom and Dad close it up and took about three months of winter off. Well, that was the original plan, but things never stay the same.

As the tourists' areas grew dad and mom couldn't stay in FL as they had in the beginning. Decisions were needed and checks signed for new merchandise. They "tightly" controlled the business and only Mom wanted to sign all large checks. When they hired David, she had him added to the account. He signed checks for monthly bills, and payroll checks only.

In late winter the large containers that had CSC Inc.'s new merchandise had docked at Charleston, SC. The trucking firm they always used needed notification. By March Gene, David and a third helper were unloading the trucks at the warehouse. Then, the rigorous process of getting it inventoried began. Stocking the ceiling-high metal shelving, so on. The business was rarely closed for more than a few weeks of the winter by the early nineties.

So the stock area could be heated Gene had put in a "torpedo" style work heater there. The last thing he did before leaving was to set the timer for about six a.m. Then, he would position it toward the vast open area. All the boxes were behind the heater. This system worked for several years.

Late one afternoon in March of 2001 someone went into the warehouse stock area. The smaller van needed loading with merchandise for delivering the next day. In getting to the boxes the heater got pushed out of the way. Then, that person forgot to reposition the heater.

David was there early that next morning, but never entered the warehouse. He had loaded the E350 van the day before. All he needed to do was jump into the driver seat and take off. Gene, sipping his coffee, looked out at the beautiful mountain view from his living room. Then, he looked down toward the warehouse and saw smoke coming from it. He dialed 911, then mom and dad.

Qualla Fire Department got there first, but proved to be ineffectual in putting out the blaze. The assistant fire chief panicked and couldn't get himself nor the crew organized. David was Fire Chief by that time, but he was in Pigeon Forge, TN.

Fortunate my parents built the warehouse close to the Cherokee Indian Reservation. The larger and more organized Cherokee Fire Department had also responded. They were the ones who put the blaze out and saved all the office machines and paperwork. My parents were forever grateful to the Native American Fire Dept. for their quick response.

Thank goodness, the company insurance covered it all. Mom called the manufacturers in China and reordered everything. The workforce moved the saved items into a large red barn. It sits across from Uncle Bill's Flea Market in Whittier. Then, she and her office helper, Bobbie started in on filing the insurance claims.

We were living in South Carolina at the time. I was in the habit of reading the Sylva Herald on line (the local weekly paper). The online edition was always a week behind, back then. No one had called me about the fire, either. Not until I saw the picture of what use to be the warehouse online.

It was late on a Friday evening when I was reading the online edition. I couldn't believe my eyes as I saw a photo of the warehouse as nothing more than a heap of smoldering twisted metal. I knew mom would be reading her Reader's Digest at about that same time. So, I called her to find out what had happened. I said we would be up the following weekend. Two weeks after the fire we visited her. My family and I stood in the parking lot and saw nothing but twisted metal, a cement slab, and steel framing. And everything still stunk!

Still in a sense of bewilderment we all went back to my parents' house and made fresh coffee. Mom didn't give out too much information at that time. It was obvious that her stress level was at its limit. She had many serious and immediate decisions to make. So, her "touchiness" was understandable. Dad has never liked the details of things, but the first to criticize. Mom had a lot on her shoulders. It was a few years later that I understood how the "pieces had always fit together" between them.

At that moment, I didn't ask too many questions. I was going through some "dark waters" myself. And I was as close to my mother as she allowed me to be. Asking her questions wasn't something I was comfortable doing.

During that time, I was suffering from a long bout of undiagnosed mild depression. I doubt I could've handled anyone else's problems at that time.

New warehouse as it looks today.

THE NEW WAREHOUSE

They worked out of the red barn for the rest of that year. When they could build the warehouse back dad did extend it from 5000 sq. ft. to 9000 sq. ft. And, yes, he added heat. By the beginning of 2002 the new warehouse was ready for them to move into it.

Left with no more than a cement slab and steel framing, he redesigned the entire warehouse. The showroom and front offices got a complete makeover. The original entrance opened to the showroom. Then the offices were along one wall.

Instead of doing that again, he changed the main entrance. It open to a wide hallway with white ceramic tile flooring. The new showroom and offices on each side of the hallway. Doing this enabled the sales person to close the door and work undisturbed with a customer. Dad lined all the front offices and showroom with birch paneling. Carpet in each room.

Each office has a row of rectangle windows that face the parking lot. At the end of the hallway dad put in a large bathroom with "wheelchair access." The stock area got its own separate bathroom. The guys took over that bathroom.

The workroom where Gene ink-stamped logos on shot glasses and lighters became larger. He used a pad printer for the printing. It's is a large machine with interchangeable parts to it. It often needs recalibrating, and he used special tools for doing this.

Gene gifted with a keen understanding of basic mechanics. He tinkered with anything having moving parts to it. Dad depended on him to keep anything mechanical maintained, and/or repaired. If Gene couldn't fix it, then it was time to call the experts in.

Dad added a separate kitchenette near the loading dock. Mom kept it well stocked with can meats, soups, and cookies. The appliances were a microwave, coffee pot, and an old Kelvinator frig.

Sometimes, my brothers and I would eat our lunch out on the dock through the summer months. It was a good time to unwind and look out at the beautiful mountain scenery.

We would sit on the side of the dock that's a few feet off the ground. One day Gene almost put his "number elevens" on a long black snake that was in the tall grass there. When he saw it at his feet he hollered, "snake" and jumped up on the dock! We followed him and jumped up to. By that time all the help had gathered to watch the creature slither down the long sloping bank away from us. It was as glad to get away from us as we were to get away from it.

WARNING SIGNS
ALWAYS WARN US

W arning signs always warn us. When we see one we should start slowing down. Same is true for life as well. There were warning signs that there was trouble in Paradise. And my mom didn't misread the signs either. But she often put what was best for the business ahead of her own personal feelings. Mom possessed an altruistic personality, to be sure.

There always seemed to be a lot at stake in keeping the warehouse up and running at full capacity. Both of my brothers gave up other jobs to work there. Later, Carol joined the sales team. She was instrumental in picking out home and kitchen decor trends at trade shows.

At first, mom and dad had hired Carol's husband Wayne. They had moved back from Virginia with their two sons. Then, about a year later Wayne quit working for my parents. Carol had divorced him about that same time. This had left a vacancy in the sales team. Carol has always had a knack for sales, so they hired her. Dad had spread his sales territory out by then. It had become too vast for one salesperson to cover.

My parents' business had become a major supplier of souvenirs throughout Southern Appalachia. But, in the middle of that my parents had their sharp differences. My mother wasn't given to speaking "double talk." Mom meant what she said and said what she meant.

This was one of Mom's strong attributes. Her impeccable honesty was another attribute. She taught us kids to take people at face value.

That's the way I still tend to think. Of course, it's easy to become "jaded." Not everyone speaks in a straightforward way.

Both my parents were controllers. They oddly had that characteristic in common. The good thing about that was that dad let mom control what she was good at. And she let him control what he was and still is good at. It worked for most of their fifty-five years of marriage.

Their working together didn't start out that way, though. Having two controlling parents did create some serious stress in my childhood home. My dad's never been one to "hold his tongue." Even, when it would've been to his favor to have kept quiet.

ROLLING STONES GATHER NO MOSS

There is an old saying that "Rolling stones gather no moss." I'm sure most everyone has heard it at least once. It's descriptive of people who can't seem to settle down. It's not meant to be derogatory in any way. Because someone can't settle down doesn't make them a bad person by any means. Often, they are the most affable people you or I will ever meet.

Still though, I'd like to rephrase that old saying. Especially since I don't know anyone who worries about moss. My rephrasing would go something like, "Rolling Stones establish no financial stability." Okay, that's not going to catch on like the original one, but it's truer than not.

My former (and deceased) brother-in-law, Wayne turned out to be a rolling stone. He and Carol met in high school. He was handsome, about 5'9." Stocky built, and played on the football team. My parents loved him from the start.

Wayne was likeable, friendly, and we all got along with him. He was the oldest of three children. His parents were "blue collar" workers. Both sets of parents liked each other.

Carol and Wayne were two "love birds" from the start. They married about a year after graduating high school. Wayne worked at a Sylva business. Carol spent that year learning drafting at the new technical school. After she completed the course, they moved to Knoxville, TN. Carol had a great job over there being a draftsman for a tractor manufacture. Everything seemed great.

Over the years though, Wayne found it hard to settle down. They, with their two sons, lived in countless places and several states. After twenty-five years of marriage Carol divorced him. This was a year or so after they moved back home.

Wayne remarried and meandered down to Myrtle Beach, SC. He sold Leaning Tree cards by then. Of course, he did well at it. They bought a condo on the beach. His sons had reconnected with him. All, seemed well.

Later, he and his wife sold the condo and bought an RV. They traveled throughout the southeast, staying on I-40 or I-95. They were wholesaling and working trade shows by then.

From there, they settled down in a rented a house in a small town in central South Carolina. By then, Wayne was no longer able to work. He was fighting a terminal illness. He needed to be near doctors who could see him on a regular basis. Settling down bought him some time and comfort.

His illness "caught up" with him, though. He passed away 2014, leaving "only his footprints" behind.

WRONGFUL ATTITUDES OR SIGNS OF DEPRESSION?

"Now I am deeply discouraged,
but I will remember you,"
—Psalms 42:6a

D uring my teenage years, I had developed some wrongful attitudes about myself. When I graduated high school in 1970 I had little sense of direction of what to do next. My grades had been mediocre and I had no real goals. Nor had I made any real decisions about anything by then.

After high school, I took drafting at our county's technical school. I failed the first year of a two-year program. So, I headed to Atlanta, GA in the fall of 1971. I had enrolled in an Art school located near Pershing Point and 17th St. I had high hopes of being a photographer.

I completed the year-long course. Photography interested me but my talent was not as big as my dreams. I became discouraged, and lost my way. I found out the hard way that it's never hard to head downward in life.

In time, I became a pot smoking hippie. Oh, I kept a regular job, working in photographic printing labs. But, I pretty much lived one day at a time. Heading in an aimless direction. I survived quite a few unwise decisions that I made during those few years.

Negative attitudes may be an early warning sign of depression. At least, that's true for me. When did I first began having depression? I don't know, I do know that I did struggle with it on and off for a long time. What started it? I'm not sure.

In 2008 I became diagnosed as having dysthymic depression. What has helped me the most in controlling it is the effective counseling I received that year. I was in my mid-fifties then. Counseling wasn't a new idea that popped into my head one day. No, I'd been to counseling before. And Jeff and I had been to marriage counseling. All the counseling was good, but had short term effects.

Somehow me having low grade depression slipped by the counselors. In the winter of 2008 I felt I needed to go back to counseling again. I picked up the phone book. I'd never seen it before, but noticed the listing for Meridian Behavioral Health Center. I called the number and described my symptoms to the front desk person. She asked if I could come right then and talk with a counselor. I said, "Sure. I'll be right there"

I'd never been to Meridian before, but had passed by it every so often. It's located here in Sylva, where I live. I met with a counselor, and we talked for at least an hour. He saw the pattern of my dark-to-light moods. That's when I first heard the term: dysthymic depression. That was his description of how I felt at times.

I attended the WRAP program they taught there. After completing that I took their other classes. I went one night a week for ten months. It was well worth my time I invested there. I've done much better at controlling my moods ever since then.

BECOMING CHRIST LIKE

"Return to me, and I will return to you,
says the LORD of Heaven's Armies."
—Zechariah 1:3b

In the spring of 1975 I began realizing I was heading down one too many dead-end roads in my life. There was a feeling of emptiness in my life. I felt that I wasn't investing my time here on Earth in wise patterns of living.

I began searching for a way out of my mess I had created. I realized that leaving my rocky lifestyle behind was only one part of life's equation. For everything we leave behind we enter a new phase of life. For me it was time to stop life's "free fall" and control my direction in life.

By early that summer I stopped all drug activity in my life. I had moved farther away from my old friends, too. I moved nearer Morningside Dr. in a beautiful old subdivision. An apartment added to an older home there, is where I lived. Every yard had pink and white dogwoods scattered throughout. Azaleas lined the houses. All the homes were brick and built during the fifties or earlier. It was a beautiful place to live. I relaxed and thought better while living there.

Moving worked out to be better for me than I realized. Not long after moving I re-dedicated my life to Jesus Christ. I had accepted Him as my Savior in my childhood. The problem was, though that I had not made Him Lord of my life. Not until then, that is.

I searched out a Christian church in my new neighborhood. And started attending there. It was a good time of spiritual growth for me. Several of the members lived near me. That made it possible for me to catch a few small Bible studies throughout the week. I attended that church for a year. After that, I entered the Air Force.

The author in 1976. My AF induction photo.

FINDING MY NICHE

I t's important that we find our niche in life. The true meaning of niche is that it is a complete environment. A place that provides all the elements needed for an organism or animal to sustain life. We understand that to mean a place where we can prosper. Each of us finding our niche is a big part of how we can achieve the American Dream.

In 1974 my sister Deena moved to Atlanta, from the Washington, DC area. We visited each other often. By 1975 she started coaxing me to join the military. Deena has always been a career minded thinker. And a great resource for ideas. I had thought about the military, but had never checked on it. That summer she convinced me to check on joining the Navy.

The Navy height requirements at that time didn't go below 5'. I'm 4'10", so the recruiter requested a height waiver for me. I waited about three months on the waiver. By then, Deena had convinced me to look at the other military branches.

I went back to the recruitment station and took the ASVAB test for the Air Force. I scored high in basic mechanics which, surprised me. I met their height requirements, as well. So, I enlisted in USAF on a delayed enlistment program. I signed up for the jet propulsion training. By May 1976 I was flying to San Antonio, Texas for Basic Training at Lackland AFB. Everything was finally falling into place for me.

After basic, I went to Chanute Air Base, Illinois for the mechanical training. There I learned how to work on the dual J-79 engines that powered the F-4 Fighter jet. I was there for six weeks.

During that time, I attended my first contemporary worship service. There was a small group of us that met in the old Chapel on Sunday morning. We sat in a circle around a large spool near the alter. A man in casual clothes bought the message. Before and afterwards we sang praise songs I'd never heard before. It was an awesome experience.

After Chanute, I went to my assigned duty station, Spangdahlem AB, Germany. Not long after getting settled in at "Spang" I got involved with the base Chapel. I was instrumental in getting a Bible Study going on Sunday morning for us young adults. There hadn't been one in a while. So, I asked my favorite Chaplain if he would lead one. Lt Col Boyles agreed to be the teacher. That one idea brought an amazing number of young adults, both married and unmarried to the Chapel. We filled the annex room.

During the Sunday worship hour, I volunteered with a friend of mine to do children's church. We did that for at least one year. In the summer, I got permission to help in VBS, then reported for duty in the afternoon. My life was good all the way around.

I met my husband Jeff, while attending the base Chapel in the Spring of 1978. Jeff's from central Georgia, and still has his soft GA accent. We both were a little older than most of the other singles in our Bible Study group. That might be why we "caught" each other's eye.

Not long after dating we felt like things had "clicked" for us. We were in love with each other. Three months later, Chaplain Boyles married us in front of about fifty guests at the Chapel.

My wedding dress was handmade by Marlene Lyons. She and her husband "Lucky" Lyons lead a popular Bible Study on Sunday nights for young adults. They were older couple raising three teenage daughters. Even with their busy lives though, they opened their home and lives to us young singles.

From there Jeff and I moved to Hill AFB, Utah. My enlistment was nearing completion. I had received the Good Conduct Medal, and was proud of my record. I received an Honorable Discharge in 1980.

By the time I received my discharge, our first child, Ruth had been born. Two years later, we had Rachel. By then, we had moved back to Germany and two years later we had Esther. After that we moved to Turkey. Life for all five of us has been good all the way around.

In 1987, Jeff received an Achievement Medal. This was for his quick action on salvaging our neighbors' base housing apt at Incirlik AB, Turkey. It flooded while they were camping. Because we shared a common wall, it almost flooded ours to!

He served during Desert Storm as did thousands of other service men and women. Jeff received an Honorable Discharge in 1994. Because of his hard work and dedication, we have reached our own American Dream.

WHO'S GOING TO BE
IN CONTROL?

As I've stated both of my parents were and are controllers. In truth, I've known many people in my life that I would describe as controllers. Some overbearing, and some not. That's not a bad characteristic to have. Leaders, need and want some control to be able to lead.

My dad lead him and Mom out of a paycheck-to-paycheck existence. He took her into a new world neither had ever experienced before 1964. They entered the world of prosperity. The world of "more than enough!"

Now there were clashes along the way. There always is when two controllers live under the same roof. Both of my parents enforced their uncompromising will upon us five children. To my mother's credit, it was she who established order as soon as she walked through the door from work. We wouldn't see Dad until after six or seven that night.

Life is not perfect. God gave us five kids the kind of Mom who not only parented single-handed. But, also her teachings to us kept all five of us out of any serious trouble throughout our lives. All five of us turned out to be honest hard working "doers." Like our mother.

It's hard to describe my dad with one or two sentences. He possesses a multi-faceted personality. I love him, but it's hard to "swallow" his criticisms. I never know if he's going to say something nice or not. Others would describe dad as a great communicator, an all-around great guy. And, sometimes he is. It's hard to "pin" his personality down in one or two sentences.

THE PLUSES AND MINUSES DO ADD UP

Over time my parents clashed over spending. My mother was always frugal. Dad was not. He seemed to enjoy going on spending sprees on buying new merchandise. His restocking the warehouse seemed to correspond with his "high positive" energy times.

Often, it worked out that dad had chosen the right new items to sell. He did have a knack for picking out "impulse buy items." He bought large quantities of merchandise. Sometimes he over filled the warehouse with it.

Doing that often worked out for them, though. A craze for a fad can sweep across America. And that means a lot of potential sales opportunities for both the whole seller and retailer.

If Dad ordered too much then, they were stuck with boxes of unsaleable stuff after the fad had died down. Granted he did "rake in" a sizeable profit by the time the fad had faded. Most any fad item has a 200% markup.

Still though, paying the tax on the overage of fad items year after year "ate" into their yearend profits. Yet, Dad would often repeat this process year after year on "fad" items. Within a few years, he would "cut a deal" with flea marketers and get rid of the leftovers at below his cost.

To curb Dad's spending sprees Mom had it set that he always needed a cosigner for the business checks. He didn't like that, so he got a business credit card without her knowledge. Of course, she found out when the bill came in the mail. The upside to getting the credit card were the air miles that dad accumulated. On one vacation, they flew to Hawaii for free.

They clashed over other things as well. But mom often "swallowed" her hurt feelings. She then moved on to do what was best for the company and kept their frazzled marriage glued together.

My dad appreciated Mom's, Gene's and Carol's input on items as well. Mom picked out all the miniature tea sets and tea pots that sold year after year. I've collected several of them for my house. She and Carol were the first to notice and acted on the "Rooster craze." I have one of the showroom roosters above my kitchen cabinets. It's a treasure to me.

To dad's credit he has always had the "gift of gab." This also, means knowing when to stop talking and let the product "sell its self." He's a "right-brain" visual thinker. He's always had the knack of knowing what the latest fad items are. Of course, he always sold tried-and-true souvenir items as well.

Carol told me how much her husband Bill had helped her and my parents. He is a retired banker and enjoyed traveling with Carol after he retired. They worked her retail customers from Maggie Valley, NC all the way to Gatlinburg, and Pigeon Forge, TN.

After doing that for a while, Bill got a catalog, some samples, and went out by himself selling. When Mom and Dad added Bill as a salesman, the company made a $1,000,000 gross profit for several years running. Even so, Mom always said no one could outsell "silver tongue" Dad.

STOP SIGNS ALWAYS MEAN STOP

S top signs always mean for us to come to a complete stop. Stop signs don't mean for us to slow down and yield or not yield. Well, the same is true in life as well. Coming to a complete stop is a good time for us to rethink things over.

At a stop sign you can pause, think, and change your direction. Finding time to close out the outside world in life is important, as well. Bringing the activity to a stop helps us to rest and "recharge our batteries." My parents' home was that place. It's a long "ranch" style brick home. With the sunroom addition, it's 2200 sq. ft. Mom loved living there as much as anyone could love their home.

The house sits on a side road in Whittier. My parents bought about 4 ½ acres in 1967 and moved our trailer there. About two acres goes up a hill. The rest of it faces the road. Part of the flat area was swampy back then. But, there was enough dry land for them to put our trailer on the lower lot.

They had the county to put a long pipe down the middle of the lot. This was to channel off a stream that the county let run onto the property when they graded and paved the road. My mother being free of the restaurant spent a lot of time moving dirt around the yard with a wheelbarrow. I didn't realize it until years later that Mom was "landscaping" all the while.

It took a while but, she covered the entire pipe with loose dirt. Much later, she had a neighbor who owned a track hoe place drainage tiles along the back half of the upper front lot. Fill dirt was next. This is where they wanted to build their house.

I graduated high school in 1970. After a year at the local technical school I left in 1971. They had not started their house plans yet. Most of the front lot was still undeveloped, back then. But by 1975 mom and dad had their dream house built. By 1980 Mom had it paid off.

In building it they took a basic 1,800 sq. ft. "ranch style" house plan and modified it. In designing it they left out a small third bedroom and made that a part of their master bedroom. In that area they made a reading nook. They did have a second bedroom and bathroom put in. The den had a foldout couch where our girls slept when we visited. Mom had Anderson roll out windows put throughout the house.

The kitchen was well lit by both the windows and the lights. Mom had an island that divided the long kitchen. A "drop in" range is there and a built-in oven is on the wall. The kitchen opens up into a roomy dining room. No doors, only archways were in the main living areas.

Dad had a beautiful (and complicated) organ in the living room. Plus, he had a piano in the den. He's always loved Lawrence Welk's "Champagne Music." He has reams of sheet music that he's collected. Plus, he's got "cheater chord" sheets that tell him where to place his fingers. He's self-taught but you'd never know it if you heard him play.

He wanted to play his organ while mom wanted to watch TV. He fixed that problem by adding a TV in their bedroom. Plus, he bought earphones for the organ.

Much later he added a large ceramic tiled sunroom onto the back. That's where we always had Christmas celebrations. Mom would put up a beautiful decorated tree there right after Thanksgiving.

Their home, among their other possessions is why she sued my dad. She wanted to live in her home in peace for the remaining years of her life. Also, mom was looking out for her children as well. She wanted her house and her possessions to go to us children. In making sure of that happening she had her lawyer to draw up a strict Will.

She had worked as hard as he did to have all that they owned. Dad never even retained a lawyer. At first, he tried his best to talk Mom out of seeing a lawyer. Then, he tried to stop her from going to court.

None of his approaches worked with Mom by that time though. Mom was resolute in her determination to claim what she felt was hers. Dad, finally asked her to please keep the business intact when it was all said and done. They both loved working at the warehouse. Three of their children worked there. There was nowhere for any of them to go by that time. Mom, herself was seventy-eight by then.

I and Carol went to court that morning to support our Mom. We both saw our seventy-eight-year-old mother take the witness stand. Mom described issues about their marriage that need to not be mentioned again.

After her testimony, the Judge ruled in my mother's favor. My mother took possession of all physical property at that moment. Dad received the inventory and company equipment.

After that they divorced each other. My parents had married over fifty-five years by that time.

It was in visiting Mom after dad moved out that I learned many things. Of course, I knew the highlights well enough. Mom being in her house was a good time for her to unwind and talk about things. She was always more pleasant to be around when she was at home brewing a fresh pot of coffee, or out in her flower garden.

THE LOVE OF A PET

I would be remiss if I didn't mention Mom's two dachshunds. The first little "hotdog" got named Pete. My family and I were gone a lot during Pete's years so I only have vague memories of him. I'm sure he was a well-loved pet, though.

The next little four-legged guy's name was Rex. He was a black and tan dachshund. One of their neighbors raised dachshunds. So, when Dad heard they had a new litter he walked up there by himself. He looked over the little newborns and picked one out. A few weeks later he walked back up and scooped up the cutest little male dog. He walked back down to the house and laid the little puppy in Mom's lap. She was swept "off her feet" with her new little four-legged boy. She named him "Rex."

A few years later Rex was having back problems. Mom and Dad stopped their work activities and took Rex all the way over to the UT School for Veterinarians. He had his back surgery, then they went back to pick him up. He was in perfect health after that. Mom made him a little pallet with an old blanket beside her side of the bed. Mom made sure he never climbed up nor jumped off furniture after his surgery.

Mom had leather interior in her car so her seats were cold. She solved that problem by putting a blanket in the passenger seat for Rex. Then, he had his little pallet at the warehouse. Rex only went where Mom went, that's for sure. He lived about fourteen years before passing away. After Rex, she couldn't bear to have another dog in her life.

MAKING THE DAYS COUNT INSTEAD OF COUNTING THE DAYS

How did my dad learn to be a successful salesman? It all started in his childhood. By the time he was thirteen, his dad had taught him everything he needed to know about sales. This included how to make the successful "cold call."

After Clyde got off work he took my dad with him to sell family Bibles door-to-door. On Saturdays, they sold advertising space on old time calendars to the store owners. Dad "soaked up" every little tidbit there was to know about sales.

It would've been wonderful if Dad had carried that "one-on-one" parenting on to us. But, it wasn't to be. It's always easy to look back and say, "my dad or mom was the best!" It's another story to look ahead and be that parent to the next generation.

To Dad's credit he's never spent his days looking back or reliving any old memories. He did tell us after his dad died he skipped school often. Finally, he quit school. His mother gave up trying to keep up with him. She got busy with a full-time job and keeping up with Dad's younger brother, Wayne.

Dad has always "colored outside the lines," and broke the rules as much as he has kept them. He's always been a self-starter, a "go getter." He's kept his focus on the future not the past. But, enough on the present to "connect a few of the dots." He's been a "bull in a china shop" when it's come to his family's feelings. Even with all that he is one of the most financial successful people that I know on a personal level.

BECOMING A SUCCESSFUL SALESPERSON

Certain skills are necessary in becoming a successful salesperson. And being a full-time salesperson means keeping those skills "sharpened." Selling is a misunderstood vocation. Selling seems easy, but I can tell you it's not. I've both seen it and done it. Selling is an "art" form of communication. Being successful at selling is a combination of certain personality qualities.

Once and awhile any of us can "luck" upon a sales deal that we've made a nice profit in. One time sales deals here and there do not make for a sales career though.

The qualities of becoming a successful salesperson are "caught" as much as "taught." I'm sure certain personalities are best for sales. I'd describe my dad as having a dominating personality. Sometimes brusque at home. But, in public he's congenial and often relatable.

Dad has kept an open mind to new ideas. He's always been a questioner, having the intuitive knack of asking the right questions.

Presentation of merchandise is an "art" form all on its own. Self-promotion is important to. My dad had only himself to promote to the "next level." I'm sure there are other important qualities as well. Throughout my book, I've included many qualities he possesses. Those are the qualities that have helped him in becoming a successful salesman. It's hard to divide between what's "caught" and what's "taught" in the shaping of anyone. I haven't tried to do that because doing so might lead me to becoming a "fault finder." That is not my goal.

My goal from the beginning is to inspire you the reader to reach for and achieve living your own American Dream. I feel like I've done that.

The one-on-one time Clyde Bell gave my dad during his childhood was valuable. So, valuable that Clyde's brief time of influence he had with my dad has proven to last a lifetime.

Dad liked the Tom's Snack job because it meant driving and meeting people. Those are two things he's always liked doing. I don't think at the time he thought he'd be good at selling. But, then again, maybe he was drawn to the sales side of the snack route like a "moth to a flame."

He had tried many other type of jobs the little town of Murphy had to offer. Mom told me once that Dad never liked standard jobs that kept him inside. Before my birth, he'd even tried being a dog catcher for Murphy.

Living in a small town didn't offer many work opportunities, anyway though. That helped the "city boy" narrow down his employment ideas. Maybe, he thought about how much he enjoyed helping his dad when they went out selling. They went door-to-door on Saturdays, which took most of the day.

The route job helped Dad realize he had a knack for sales. He worked at arranging and promoting his snack display to increase sales. Dad's true selling genius is in selling impulse items. As his sales increased he began to feel successful. His confidence got built up.

By the mid-fifties, we moved to Asheville. Dad had found a restaurant equipment company that needed a salesman. He was to travel throughout Western North Carolina selling to schools, restaurants, tiny cafes, and so on. He did that for about seven years. He wore out a good running used car about every other year in that job.

About 1958 we moved to the rural community of Fairview. Mom wanted to leave the suburbs of West Asheville. She became employed at a small factory in Fairview that made copper coil resisters.

By 1964 we moved to the Cherokee Indian Reservation. By 1967 my parents had established their wholesale souvenir company, CSC Inc. Taking this bold step proved to be profitable for them.

My dad's natural ability of selling impulse sales items was a success. He persuaded the shop owners to buy dozens of most everything he sold. He suggested displaying ideas, spending time with each owner.

Becoming a successful salesman didn't "fall into my dad's lap." Along the way, he tried selling several items that failed. But, he sold more profitable items, than not. Plus, I noticed he read books on sales, keeping a positive attitude, so on.

When he bought their first RV, he and Mom were influencing the local souvenir business. One good idea built on another good idea. This is how both of my parents achieved living their American Dream.

HOW BIG IS YOUR AMERICAN DREAM?

The American Dream comes in all shapes and sizes. It's potential reaches people of all different races and ethnicities. The well-educated may have a better chance than the under-educated. But, then there are gifts of talent, skills, craft abilities. These are not always measured in a classroom setting. But, that's a good place for us to discover that we have these "gifts."

Living the American Dream has much to do with honesty, and integrity. Realizing that we are the leaders of our own personal lives is important. Always question other people's influence over you.

Achieving the American Dream includes ingenuity, sometimes luck, but always ambition. The American Dream's only boundaries are the limits we put on ourselves. Also, needless to say, are our physical shore and land boundaries. I know the American Dream can happen here in America for those who strive for it. I've both seen it and experienced it.

IN MEMORY OF MY MOTHER

"You have tested my thoughts and examined
my heart in the night.
You have scrutinized me and found
nothing wrong.
I am determined not to sin in what I say."
—Ps. 17:3

I wrote this story to honor the memory of my mother, June Lloyd Bell, May 17, 1926-December 4, 2009. I loved my mother, and respected her as much as is possible. As I've grown older I appreciate all that she did for us more and more.

My mother grew up on a farm, until she left to attend Knoxville Business School in Knoxville, TN. When my siblings and I were growing up every so often mom would tell us kids about the hard work of farming. The whole family would be up early to get the farm chores done before school. Sometimes they woke up in a cold house on a snowy morning because the fire had died down in the night.

One of their older brothers had to carry in a bucket of cold water from the well. And tried not to get "soaked to the bone" in the process. Of waiting for the fire in the wood stove to get stoked back up so they could all have a hot breakfast. And yes, they had an "out house."

During the school year mother and her siblings walked a mile to school each school day. They used empty clean metal lard buckets to carry their lunch in. Their lunches of fried "side meat" with cornbread or biscuits.

During the summer, they helped Granny put together a big lunch in the morning. They packed it up to take with them when they farmed. Nobody took time to go back to the house until the work was done.

My mother learned many lessons about life growing up. Some were "caught and some taught." She learned not to let fear override her common sense. One afternoon when I was visiting with her, I saw a small snake slither onto the brick patio. The heat alone could've killed it. But, I jumped up and pointed to it. My mother, who was about eighty then, got up and grabbed her garden hoe. In one swift move, she killed the slithering little creature.

Between her genetics, her "caught and taught" values, Mom realized she'd had enough. Enough of my dad's "double talk" and broken promises. Mom sued my dad for ownership of all the physical property in 2007. This included their brick home, with 4.5 acres, and the blue warehouse with the 3.5 acres. She won, of course.

Mom forming her lawsuit caused some turmoil. But, by the time of the court hearing Dad had decided to not put up a legal fight. He knew he wouldn't win in court. Even so, both of my parents worked together every day. They worked side-by-side as they always had done. My mother worked a few hours each day up until a few weeks before her passing.

After Mom won, she had her lawyer change her Will to list only her children as heirs. We five inherited all that my mother owned.

Selling my mother's house proved to be a little difficult. My brother Gene was Mom's Executer. It took us almost two years to "pry" his grip loose on Mom's house. But, we finally did, and sold it at fair market value. Today, I still share ownership of the warehouse with my three living siblings. We all decided to let Dad continue operating CSC Inc. long as he wanted to.

This is a story that might've broken some had they lived through it. My mother was a strong woman, though. One reason she stayed strong through it all was because of her strong belief in God. She knew that she alone would be accountable for her own actions, not anyone else's. No matter what was happening in their marriage or business. And Mom determined to not be guilty of wrong doing. That is how she lived her entire life.

Because of her strong Christian faith Mom is now resting in her eternal mansion. She has a beautiful view of the Crystal Sea. (Revelation 4:6)

HONORING MY DAD

"For this is how God loved the world:
He gave his one and only Son, so that everyone
who believes in him will not perish but have eternal life."
—John 3:16

I, also wrote this to honor my Dad. He was born in Knoxville, TN on October 5, 1924. His father Clyde Bell created a lot of stress in his family. Dad's mother told my mother that Clyde had a divisive personality. That she had spent a lot of her early married years trying to keep emotional "storms" from brewing.

They were always "crammed" into small apartments with their growing family. But, living there did save my grandma Bell's life. One day when she was by herself in the apt Grandma started going into premature labor with my dad. Neighbors heard her screaming in pain and got her to the hospital in time for a safe delivery.

When Dad joined the Marines, he stationed at Newfoundland. His job was being a supply clerk. Having steady hours enabled Dad to get his GED while there. After his discharged he went back to Knoxville. That's when he and Mom met.

Grandma Bell was happy when Dad and Mom married. She saw Mom as being a "helpmate" who would help Dad live a practical and settled life.

Dad has brought both him and my mom happiness throughout their marriage. When their business was small he and mom took the RV down to Florida. Every year they would spend a few of the winter months there. Dad took the lead whether in forming their business or planning a vacation.

After the lawsuit, my parent divorced. My dad remarried shortly afterwards. All that took place in 2007. Dad will be 92 in October 2016. As of this writing he is bringing Cherokee Sales Inc. to a close.

In March 2016 Gene passed away. He had turned sixty-nine by a few days. But, even without him, CSC Inc. was in full production for about one more year. Carol, her grandson Dillon, and David are helping to bring it to a close.

A few years ago, Dad turned ninety. My oldest daughter Ruth and her boyfriend, Dennis Downey threw him a big birthday party at their house that weekend. It was a total surprise!

My Uncle Wayne came, along with several of my cousins from Knoxville. I hadn't seen any of them in more than a decade. We all had a blast getting reacquainted with each other.

I'm thankful that both of my parents raised us five to believe in God. In my childhood, we attended the nearest Baptist church in our community. We were faithful in our church and Sunday School attendance during those years. My dad is still faithful in his church attendance and tithing.

Both of my parents kept us in church throughout my childhood. We all received our own Bible in our youth. We three girls were baptized at Fairview Baptist Church. We've stayed active in our Christian faith through most of our lives.

IN APPRECIATION TO MY AUNT JO

"I was glad when they said to me,
'Let us go to the house of the LORD.'"
—Psalms 122:1

My deepest appreciation goes to my Aunt Jo Shinlever. She has shared with me many of the details of, "The American Dream." Aunt Jo still remembers hoeing corn as a small child with her own small hoe. It was my mom's job to keep up with her little sister because the adults had hoed at a quicker pace. The girls usually didn't see them until they had reached the end of the row. Then, they all would pick beans, or one of the adults would kill a chicken for dinner.

I'm forever grateful for my Aunt Jo's generosity of sharing her memories. Also, for her hospitality and wonderful cooking. She always has a wonderful meal ready for us on our visits. Visiting her has always been a pleasant experience. Her mind is as sharp today as it's ever been. She's a true joy to visit with.

My oldest daughter Ruth usually goes with me to visit with Aunt Jo. After we've had a wonderful meal, then we spend a few hours talking about anything that comes to our minds. There has never been a "set agenda."

Aunt Jo has stayed strong in her Christian faith. She has been a long-time member and Sunday School teacher in her church in Knoxville.

SECTION IV

Me, Esther, Rachel, Gene, and Cream our poodle.

"For I know the plans I have for you," says the Lord.
"They are plans for good and not for disaster,
to give you a future and a hope."
—Jerimiah 29:11

WORKING FOR MY PARENTS: NOT AN EASY TASK

My nerves became "rattled" while working for my parents at the warehouse. One day it came to me how dysfunctional my extended family had become. Well, I didn't grow up in the most emotional balance home, from the start. And time had not change family dynamics either.

In the Spring of 2007 I started ten months of counseling at a mental health facility. It's called Meridian Behavioral Health Clinic. It's located here in Sylva, NC. That was during my second year of being seasonal help at the warehouse. After Labor Day of that year I'd had enough so I quit.

I continued visiting with Mom at her home. She lived by herself by that time. Our visits were usually pleasant. It was those visits that I learned a lot of what I've written here. I moved away when I was nineteen, to Atlanta, GA. My husband Jeff and I moved back to the mountains in 2003.

Fortunate for my mom that in 2008 my sister Deena and her husband Jude Long move in with her. They had relocated to be near Mom. They hadn't sold their house in GA yet so "near" meant them moving in with her. Mom was in her late seventies by that time and becoming frail. She needed Deena's daily help with household chores and watering her flower beds. It didn't take much to make Mom agitated, but they "pressed on," and helped as much as possible. Deena and Jude, of course still worked full time jobs also during this time.

L-R: Our oldest daughter Ruth, Mom, and me on front
row. Deena, Jude, and Jeff on back row. Mid-2000.

OVERCOMING DEPRESSION

"For though I fall, I will rise again.
Though I sit in darkness,
the Lord will be my light."
—Micah 7:8b

When I started receiving counseling at Meridian it wasn't only because I worked at the warehouse. The counselor helped me to understand I was suffering from long-term mild depression. This type is Dysthymic, (aka clinical) depression. I love my parents and family but, I realized I needed to quit working there. I also, needed to stop my life long tendency to be a "fixer" and a "pleaser."

It was from those counseling sessions that I began journaling. It took a few more years to "gel" in my thoughts about using my journals to write a self-help book. In 2013 I finished writing all I could think of how I've broken negative patterns of thought. I titled my book, <u>My Journey in Overcoming Chronic Dysthymic Depression</u> (Crossbooks).

I went to both individual and group counseling for three months. After that I continued going to group counseling one evening a week. I attended several series of classes during this time. One series I loved the most is, "WRAP." I even took the Peer Support leadership classes. The time I invested in developing good mental health is still reaping rewards for me. Overcoming depression, and staying that way has become one of my personal goals

WRITING "LIVING THE AMERICAN DREAM"

"This is the day the LORD has made.
We will rejoice and be glad in it."
—Psalms 118:24

I wrote this story to inspire others to achieve their American Dream. Like my parents' generation did after winning WWII. We continue to reach the "American Dream" because of the "trails" they blazed for us. My grandparents' generation taught us to "make do" with what we have. That's because they lived through the Depression and did live that way. They knew how to bring a full life together with so few "ingredients."

I'm thankful that I've had many relatives who persevered through hardships, but still endured. Life is not always a "bed of roses" my mother would often say. But still, they reached levels of prosperity they never in the beginning thought were possible.

Of course, none were flawless. Some more flawed than others. But I'm not here on Earth to pass my judgements. I don't believe that's God's will for me. I wanted my opinions to "take a back seat" in writing the "Dream." I've achieved that goal in as much as it is possible for me to do so.

I'm not a note taker. I write from memory and personal experience. I've never even thought about bringing all these stories together into one story. Not until I rewrote this one from a short story I started about a year back. That one was just about my parents creating their business, CSC Inc.

I couldn't write for long on this story, though. Writing this personal account has been an emotional journey for me. A "journey" that's included a "healing" on some level on almost every page I've written. I hope I've helped you to receive a healing of events from your past. None of our lives are "wrinkle free." None of us can change the past. We can change the future, though.

During the summer of 2016 I began a "stream of consciousness" about this unique and personal story. An experience I had not felt before about it. Once I started rewriting it I couldn't keep up with my thoughts, they would come so quick. I realized that many of my family members have or are living their American Dream.

Weaving all the stories and brief accounts together to be as accurate as possible has been one of my goals. Also, I wanted to treat each one with the love and respect I have for them. I have done my best to write the truth as I've heard it or as I became an eye witness to it.

Yet, I didn't want it to be a "blab-it-all" book. My mother was private about her life. And about the deep issues that divided her and Dad. In moving back home, of course I saw plenty enough myself. Not much of that would've inspired anyone at any time. My goal was and is to honor both of my parents. I've reached that goal throughout my book.

One thing I've realized more so in writing this story is how brief our lives are. That's why it's important for us to make the days count rather than count the days. Oh, I'm not talking about children counting the days till Christmas or their birthday. I'm thinking more so about the fact that we only get one day at a time. We're not promised tomorrow. Today is the day we start turning our dreams into reality. From here we can sow a legacy that will continue through the generations.

I'm proud to say that my older relatives did make each of their days, count and continue to do so. My Uncle Charles attended UT in the 1940's. He established a legacy of how important education is to his three daughters. Then, on to the third generation. Today he and my Aunt Jo have a granddaughter that has graduated Harvard. She has gone on to receive a Fulbright Scholarship. That's legacy of education and accomplishment to be proud of.

THE UNBROKEN CIRCLE

My parents five children have kept up with one another through the years. At present, three of us with our spouses live in Jackson County, NC. Our sister Carol lives in Buncombe County, which is nearby. As I've mentioned, my brother Gene recently passed away. We four surviving siblings own the blue warehouse that sits on a hill overlooking US 441. Gene left his fifth share to his sisters. And, we'll soon be selling the warehouse.

You might ask why isn't the prosperous business CSC Inc. being passed down to the next generation? It was never designed for passing on to us. Neither of my parents desired to train their children to take it over. They never relinquished any level of control of it over to us.

By late fall of every year dad had drained the company's checking account down to all but the minimal. Some of this money went into their IRA accounts. Mom also, had an annuity. There never was profit sharing. But the employees did receive a small bonus each December. Bill never received a bonus even though he was on the payroll. They may have listed Bill as Carol's employee (like a sub-contractor).

When my dad calls, it quits then that'll be the end of CSC Inc. That's the way both of my parents wanted it. It's been an amazing journey. Both sad and wonderful events have happen over it's some fifty-plus years of being a business.

Even so, the circle of family, faith, and hard work has widened, but is still strong. My husband Jeff and I have three daughters who have and continue to bless us. Our oldest daughter Ruth works in the mental health field since graduating USC, Columbia SC. She then, went on to get her Masters in counseling. Today she, her boyfriend Dennis Downey, and their two cats live near us.

Ruth and I have certain things that we enjoy doing together. One of those is to visit my Aunt Jo who lives in Knoxville, TN, about two hours away. Ruth and I try not to let too much time go by between our visits with Aunt Jo. Ruth takes a "comp" day from work to go with me. It's a nice visit all the way around. And a good break for her. I try to keep our travel communication "light" unless we need to talk about something.

Our middle daughter, Rachel started her work life with a good job. At the time, she married and had her family as well. But, when she became a single mom, Rachel realized she had more potential than what her job required. She felt "boxed in."

That was Rachel's impetus to "shift her paradigm." She was a single mom in her early thirties when she enrolled at Western Carolina University. (WCU is near us here in Jackson County.)

Rachel and her two daughters, Mia and Isabelle moved in with us during that time. She had some college credits that WCU accepted. Two years later she graduated with a BS in Accounting. Now Rachel has a great career in the banking field, and they live in the piedmont section of NC.

Our youngest daughter, Esther lived with us on and off during her twenties. She too married then divorced during that time. When "Es" lived with us she graduated Southwestern Community College with an A. A.

"Es" has always gone to the beat of a different drum. One day, "outta tha' blue" she decided to move across America to the L. A. area. Within a year or so she landed a great job doing copy editing for a national business there. "Es" keeps a blog, rides her bicycle to work, and in general enjoys the Southern CA lifestyle.

Jeff retired after twenty years in the US Air Force. He got his CDL and now enjoys a career in the trucking industry. He trains those that want to be truck drivers.

In my forties, I attended Coker College, Hartsville, SC. I graduated in 2000 with a Sociology Degree. I enjoyed taking the college courses. After graduating I worked in social work, both in SC and in NC. It made me depressed, so I quit working in that field.

My sister Deena met her husband, "Jude" (James) Long in the Atlanta area. They married and raised their two children, Jacob and Bonnie in Bartow County, GA. Jacob graduated Carson-Newman College, TN. He married and lives near where my dad grew up in Knoxville, TN. He and his wife Erin are living in and restoring an older home there. Bonnie, lives in east Tennessee.

My brother, David and his wife Janice have two grown children that live nearby. Jeremy, their son is a long-time employee at Harrah's Casino. He married his high school sweetheart, Tasha and they have three young children.

David and Janice's daughter Angie married her high school sweetheart, Jamie. They have two children. Angie graduated WCU with a degree in Social Work. She worked in that field until her grandson was born. He was born with Spinal Muscular Atrophy (SMA). To give him all the care he needs Angie resigned from her job to take care of him.

Carol and her first husband Wayne have two sons. Wayne C. Shuler II worked in the construction field, but passed away a few years ago. Grayson, their youngest son has his CDL and drives local.

My oldest brother M. Eugene "Gene" Bell married and then divorced six months to the day later. They had no children. Gene, smoked throughout his adult life. In 2015 he developed bone cancer because of that habit. During the next year, Carol divided her time between him, her husband Bill, and her job at CSC Inc. In appreciation of her sacrifice to help him out as much as possible he left his house to her. Today, Grayson lives in the tidy 900 sq. ft. house.

Weaving all these personal accounts together has made me realize that it's the doers who "point the way." The achievers, "light the way." Those that dawdle most always walk right by the "door of opportunity." Maybe, they're waiting for someone to open it for them.

Mistakes happen, but we shouldn't let the fear and anxiety of that hold us back. We all are only here for a set number of days. None of us know how many days we have. What we are in charge of is what we do with the time that we have here on Earth. My hope is that you're inspired in reading this to reach for and live your American Dream.

AUTHOR'S NOTE

Having hope will give you courage.
You will be protected and will rest in safety.
—Job 18:11

In closing, I've included many good attributes my dad has that's made him a successful entrepreneur. We all have a certain niche that's right for us. My dad's drawn to selling like "a moth to a flame." He was in his late twenties by the time he started his snack route. Something in him "clicked" then, and he never stopped selling thereafter.

My parents' road to entrepreneur success included some unplanned "weigh stations," though. That's where they were somewhat forced to get rid of their accumulated "baggage." Difficult situations that marred some of their lives together. It was at those places they had to face the truths that were separating them as a couple and as business partners.

Fissures in their foundation crumbled their marriage and almost destroyed their business. None of us can ignore the fissures for long. It's the way life is, if we're to live in honesty and truth. This is what my mother lived by, and it served her well.

I've closed their story with a devotion that came to me one day while writing this book. It describes who they were and are as individuals. Although, it can apply to all at some point in our lives.

Thank you for reading my book. As I've said in the beginning feel free to let me know if you've enjoyed reading "Living the American Dream."

WHEN YOU'RE BETWEEN A ROCK AND A HARD PLACE START CHISELING!

When we're between a rock and a hard place, God gives
us the "tools" to start chiseling away at our problems.
With our prayers, He wants us to carve a beautiful
piece of sculptured art from our rock of problems.
The hammer hitting the chisel represents our pain, and tears.
We all have problems that are too big for us to solve on our own.
Our prayers go up to Heaven at odd hours of the night. They
chisel away the heaviness of our hearts over our problems.
Sometimes, we can win a "battle" with our own
reasoning. But we may end up losing the "war" of the
bigger problem with our short-sightedness.
Oh, we think, "I can solve this one on my own," and not
bother asking for God's help, nor ask for help at all.
God loves and cares for us. He's waiting for us to call upon Him.
He always sends answers to our prayers from
the heavens when we seek Him.
An ancient king, named David had his own troubles. But, he
wrote some reassuring words that are still true for us today:

"For he will conceal me there when troubles come;
He will hide me in his sanctuary.
He will place me out of reach on a high rock." Psalms 27:5

Printed in the United States
By Bookmasters